As sparks fly upward

As sparks fly upward

The rationale of the Farm and Wilderness Camps

Kenneth Webb

PHOENIX PUBLISHING • Canaan, New Hampshire 03741

Copyright 1973 by Phoenix Publishing

Printed in the United States of America
by Courier Printing Company
Binding by New Hampshire Bindery
Design and illustration by A. L. Morris

Library of Congress Catalog Card Number 73-90087
ISBN 0-914016-04-0

To My Wife

Susan Howard Webb

With All My Love

. . . and the realization that most of the
following would have been impossible
without her practicality, her patience,
her sensitivity and her ability to live with
a determined entrepreneur.

Contents

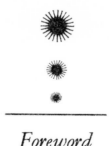

Foreword

When a request came from the American Camping Association to write a monograph on the implications for organized camping of the rugged, simple type of environment the Farm and Wilderness Camps exemplify, I turned to some of the ideas in the growing manuscript of *As Sparks Fly Upward*, stating frankly that I would adapt portions of the larger work to the purposes of that monograph.* The heart-warming reception accorded it argues that this present book, reflecting as honestly as a necessarily subjective appraisal can the many aspects of these camps, may in the same way "speak to our condition," as the Quaker phrase goes. Although this started as a simple history of the camps and a discussion of what their social significance may be, the swift pace of somber events in our nation has supplied a larger canvas and a more urgent theme.

In our nation's present crisis, it becomes evident that the cause of its deep malaise can be reached only through the more honest approach and the penetrating insights of the new generation. Despite superficial appearances, these insights are deeply religious, the sort of idealistic, unself-seeking spiritual commitment which our country must have if it

Summer Camps: Security in the Midst of Change, American Camping Association, Bradford Woods, Martinsville, Indiana 46151.

is to be saved — the sort of commitments which are fostered in the straightforward, friendly atmosphere of a good camp.

As the Government begins to recognize the importance of "Camping for All," and moves to make this long-cherished dream of the camping movement a reality, many of the ideals the Farm and Wilderness Camps have tried to implement — integration, for instance; work as education; ruggedness and simplicity; the primacy of spiritual values; the deep social concern which is the essence of true patriotism — become relevant to the larger framework.

Mostly through trial and error in attempting to implement convictions deeply held, these camps seem to have achieved a certain flexibility and durability, related qualities which may help steer them through the contradictions of the present age. Because of this flexibility, guided nevertheless by principles which are the same always, these camps seem to be able to speak to the modern age.

For a generation often uncertain, the Camps have frequently given purpose to life, sometimes a Quaker social concern, sensitive, understanding, creative. In an era of alienation, they elicit full involvement. In place of self-indulgence, they offer work, meaningful, diverse, often grubby; instead of competition, cooperation; for boredom, the challenge of new skills, far mountains and distant water-ways. To reduce confusion, the healing silences of the daily Meeting for Worship.

To older campers groping for individual identity, the Camps have often brought self-understanding, awareness of the relation of individuals to each other, to their environment, and to some type of spiritual reality. A system of values, consciously accepted, can undergird a sound and unshakable spiritual strength which it is possible to build on the current destruction of traditional values. The new generation often has the modern type of respect which results from freely accepted new and honest values. Their hall-mark is reverence for all life.

"How do you handle such or such a problem?" some young camp director asks my wife or me. We may have found one way the issue can be handled, but we are unable to answer until we consider the practice in question and try to put into words the underlying principle which may then be applicable to another situation.

I hope the following pages will not seem in any way smug or self-satisfied. This would be ironical in the face of our realization that (1) we have just begun to tap the rich potential for social betterment which camping provides, (2) we know we don't have all the answers, and (3) others have experimented also with many of these values and have often gone further than we, so that these pages should set forth something of a composite of Things That Have Worked.

But in the interest of presenting a unified and readable account of how certain fundamentals may be implemented, we offer this frank picture of our own set of camps with bits here and there borrowed from other camps which are blazing similar trails.

May the trails described in these chapters prove inviting not only to other camping people, both directors and staff, but to educators in general, who may find valid principles of education set forth in different guise; to psychologists, who may be interested to see how nonprofessional psychologists (camp directors) approach certain problems; and to parents — who must be true psychologists to be successful. May this book prove to be of value also to Quakers and to all others concerned for the spiritual health of our youth; to all who work with children and realize that you can't just treat the symptoms; to all true lovers of our country, who find patriotism to be far more than raising a flag and reciting a pledge. Finally, perhaps the kids themselves will like to read this book, if only to see whether it's just another of Holden Caulfield's "phonies." A warning to Farm and Wilderness campers: you won't find yourself or your friends in these pictures. To try to identify individuals in these pages should be entertaining but also frustrating, for these characters for the most part are composites, like characters in fiction. As such, they may be truer to life than life itself.

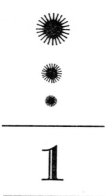

1

The "Bishop Mowing"

In the Green Mountains of Plymouth Township in Central Vermont, an expanse of upland meadow and pasture land overlooks a valley to the west. In that valley lies a lake rimmed with birches, evergreens and maples. Beyond the lake, wooded slopes rise again toward the long ridge that becomes Killington.

The last few centuries have wrought many changes. Originally the slopes were heavily wooded. Then came the settlers. They built a road above the shores of the pond, a road which became part of the stage-coach route from Montreal to Boston. Before the coaches gave way to rails along the Connecticut River, the settlers had felled much of the original timber and divided the land into farms.

A family named Bishop settled on the plateau along the old stage-coach road. A spring of water cold as ice served the barn above the road and bubbled on down to the old weather-beaten farmhouse across the way. Unpainted it would have been, with narrow gray clapboards set off in the summer by a riot of orange day lilies with lilac bushes at the corners. An ancient apple tree or two, probably the old Tinmouth, a local variety, would have leaned over the dooryard.

The pungent smoke of apple wood drifts from the kitchen chimney.

An exhilarating autumn fragrance comes from the open door, an aroma compounded of apples cooking on the stove, of peppers, spices, of butternuts and brown sugar all simmering and bubbling together to add to that delightful concoction known as mincemeat.

A matronly woman stands in the doorway, her plump arms wrapped in the folds of an apron. With narrowed eyes she studies the pasture land tilted above her across the road. Hurried along by a barefooted girl with pigtails, a half-dozen cows are winding their way down toward the barn. The "swing-paced cattle," the same in Homer's time, the same forever.

A man and a half-grown boy are busy in the farmyard, bringing in shiny milk pails from the rack on which they have been drying in the sun. Several children race about, the youngest keeping well to the lea of an old gander. An older boy paces a frisky calf. Half pulled by the animal, he shouts his delight. Into the yard turns a team of dapple grays, bringing a load of cornstalks for the stock. The sound of the creaking wheels can be heard above the honking of the geese and the shouts of the boy with the calf.

At that time, and in fact, until almost the turn of the century, the pasture land above the house skirted the woods of the steeper slopes. Below it on the gentler grades a broad expanse of hayland ran down to the hedgerow that fringed the road. After the old house disappeared, its lonely site was marked by a crumbling cellar hole and the wild tangle of day lilies struggling among lilacs and seedling apples. But the great sweep of hayland above, still known as the Bishop Mowing, was cut each year by neighboring farmers. And in its lower corner the unfailing spring of clear cold water — the Bishop spring — still slaked the thirst of sturdy farm boys hot and sweaty from haying.

As the economy of the state continued to change in the early decades of the nineteen hundreds, the sons of these farm boys left the land. The Bishops' fertile acres lay neglected. Poplar seedlings and their cousin, the white birch, invaded the old pasture. Maples and chokecherries and wild apples advanced into the hay land from the woods around its edges. The Bishop spring bubbled on unnoted.

Then another and more striking change began in the middle decades of the century. Tangles of timothy and clover, hardhack and black-eyed susan had crowded out the earlier mowing; now these gave way to garden. And below the garden an assortment of coops and open shelters, their frequently lopsided construction suggesting youthful builders, springs up in the erstwhile mowing. There are several small coops for hens. The pigpen at the top of the area is big enough, but several of the stubby posts have had to be propped. The goat shelter, a space for sheep, and the calf pens are bisected by a rivulet from a small spring in the woods. This source, besides furnishing a supply of water for the afore-mentioned goats and calves, is painstakingly fenced from four-legged in-trusion for most of its course. At the lower end of this runnel the water is caught in a cement basin in which flourishes a trio of ducks. At one side a flight cage has been set up. A whir of wings and a spread of white tail call a visitor's attention to several king pigeons and a pair of bobwhite who share these quarters more or less amicably.

This is the Timberlake Farm, part of the Farm and Wilderness Camps. A new crop of boys, younger than the sturdy farmers' sons who hayed the Bishop Mowing, are getting their feet into the warm soft earth of the ancient tillage. They are learning the peculiar ways of calves and pigs and goats, ways that are the same in all generations. Much more are they discovering than the way a calf will nuzzle its mother, and the strange little cluck with which a mother hen summons her brood when a hawk planes the air currents down from the timbered ridge.

The transformations taking place in these youngsters of a new age may not be so apparent to a casual observer as are the changes in the Bishop Mowing. But they are even more significant. These are city chil-dren, most of them deprived by their environment of the challenge and the hardship by which country boys grew strong and self-reliant. Though their urban horizons are broader, their character often lacks the honest self-esteem which comes of conquering difficulties; the confidence of knowing that one is needed; the determination which results from having to find a way to do a job and discovering that one can.

Psychologists tell us that self-confidence is built on self-respect, which in turn results from a sense of being needed. In previous genera-tions leaders in the professions and in business and industry often came from farms like that of the Bishops. Starting from their tenderest years, the Bishop children all had chores to do. If this work was not done, the whole family suffered. The contribution of even the youngest was, there-fore, recognized as necessary to the smooth operation of the little world of which each child felt himself securely a member. This sense of be-longing and of being needed generated its own self-esteem. A sense of security was the result. It is the lack of this sense of security which produces many of the vague fears and anxieties of the present day. And this lack, so psychologists tell us, fathers many of the ills our minds are heir to.

Daily chores with their indirect blessing were not the only benefit of this simple, rugged life. Besides keeping the woodbox full, or sweeping out the storage shed every day, or helping set the table and do the dishes, or feed the calves, a child might often choose to have livestock of his own to care for. If not a calf or a cosset lamb, it might be rabbits or bantams which taught him many lessons besides the primary one of responsibility.

These city youngsters who man the TL Farm are learning some of these lessons. They are absorbing so much so fast that this bit of land wrested a second time from the wilderness may truly be said to be enchanted, if enchantment means, as the *Oxford Dictionary* states, "Invested with magical powers or properties." A knowledgeable visitor would pick up much of what is happening here; the trained eye of the educator would see its full significance.

In general the area of the camp farm is strictly functional. The disordered set of homemade coops and hutches can hardly be termed "neat." Their fences run from hither to yon with scant regard for regularity. The sole aim is to keep the stock *in*. The fencing doesn't always serve even that purpose.

This group of boys, for instance, with their butts sticking up along the lower edge of the feedhouse at the TL farm: they are in process of learning something which can apply to larger worlds. The owners of the rearends are bent double, peering into the murky gloom underneath the feedhouse floor in search of a rabbit that has got out.

One of the boys, hearing a chuckle behind him, raises up on his knees to see a bent figure in faded overalls looking down at the line of boys. It is Clayton Fish, the old Vermont farmer in charge of this "menagerie."

"Alexander is out again," the boy says to the newcomer.

"And we — we *think* Scheherazade is there too and maybe they're mating." Another head had appeared from under the shed.

The chuckle is followed by a broad grin. "That'll be an interesting mix: a Dutch-belted father and a Belgian hare mother."

"But we couldn't help it. They got out." A third boy raised up to turn his eyes toward the stocky form of the farmer.

The latter chuckled again. " 'Course you can't help it *now*. But you could a kep' 'em from a-gitt'n' out so much."

"How?" the boys chorused.

"Come over here and I'll show you."

The quartet trooped after the farmer. "If'n you want to have the does loose in one big pen, which is fine for them, either you put wire under the hull run — then the poor critters can't git no grass to eat — or you dig down a foot all round the fence and sink another roll of wire in the ground. A rabbit'll dig out if he can. That's his nature."

The four spent the morning digging a ditch along the perimeter of the rabbit yard and installing a roll of one-inch mesh one foot deep. This mighty undertaking held the little animals for several days. Then one morning the boys came up to feed their charges and found about half of them gone. Examination showed a hole between the upper fence and the subterranean addition.

"Well, you gotta be thorough," the old farmer commented, when the boys showed him the new hole. "Somebody skipped a foot or so of fence along here in tying the upper and the lower rolls together. See, here's another place they'll be a-gitt'n' out in a few days. And here's one. Hafta go all along here and tie 'em together better."

"But we can't stay up here this morning," one of the boys protested. "There's some distance tryouts at the water front this morning and I want to be in them."

"And I've got to be in the garden. Whole cabin's going up there this morning," another objected.

The old farmer knew boys as well as rabbits. Painstakingly checking the wire along the whole length of the fence was almost like paying for a dead horse. The digging job had been done; the first flush of enthusiasm was over. While campers might learn a lesson in thoroughness by going back over their work, boys of this age might also lose interest in rabbits.

"I tell you what to do," he offered. "You feed 'em up real good this morning. Put in some extry clover for them. That'll keep 'em busy a while. Then come up here tomorrow and we'll swing a new fence clear out around that little knoll where the clover's so thick. Figure it out for yourself: if'n you was a rabbit, wouldn't you quit diggin' for a while if you had more'n you could eat right where you was, and plenty of room to run around?"

While the farmer helped the boys build their bigger pen the next day, he took precautions to cover himself in case this new suggestion didn't work.

"If'n an animal has all he wants to eat and plenty of space to run, he won't generally git out. But rabbits is ornery sometimes."

In another week the man had occasion to recall this sage pronouncement.

"I didn't think they'd git out any more, but you know I said they wouldn't *generally* git out. Now and then they do. Rabbits is ornery."

"What do we do now?" one of the boys asked. "We've tried everything."

"Well, no you ain't, not quite. You've got the bucks now in separate wooden hutches where they can't dig. You've got wire around the main part of the big run, and you've built on an extension for the ones that's got big appetites. Now here's a different kind of an idea. You notice when the does git out, Kim Hanson don't never have no trouble with his does going under the shed? Know why? Kim makes pets of his rabbits, and they just come hoppin' up to him. No hiding under the shed for them. Why not make pets of all them rabbits? Just spend a little extry time with them, pettin' them and a-feeding them out of your hand. See how soft their fur is. They's lots that's interestin' about a rabbit."

Here was a new approach. Like life itself, you had a problem. You tried a solution. It didn't work. You tried another way. Also not a sure cure. Then you discovered a radical new approach, and the problem disappeared. In this instance, the type of solution applied to rabbits suggested something about ways of solving problems with people.

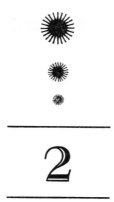

2

" . . . There's swagger in my step"

The first hike ever taken from camp was the memorable trip to Stratton Pond in the southern part of the state. This was in the rainy summer of 1938, a summer that resulted in the "1938 flood" to pay for which Vermonters got an extra item on their tax bill for the next ten years.

Timberlake, first of the Farm and Wilderness Camps, began in 1939, under the name of Mehrlicht, which nobody could understand over the telephone. In the summer of 1938 I was running a large day camp near Buffalo, New York. With a station wagon load of boys and another counselor, I drove to Vermont for a week's exploration of the area. It was impossible to understand why a spot so ideally suited to a boys' camp hadn't been snapped up before: there must be something wrong about it which everybody else was bright enough to see. Each day revealed new delights in the location. The week convinced the explorers that there was no hidden defect.

One difficulty did become evident, however: it rained. Every day. Some days it didn't just rain, it poured. You couldn't blame that on the location, for it was raining everywhere in Vermont. The group from Buffalo had set up camp in the Catamount Clearing, the same spot where in the previous century the Bishops' house had stood, whence Mrs. Bishop had scanned the slanting hillside pasture from the kitchen doorway.

The expedition from Buffalo decided tents were useless in such rain, so they cut posts to put in a wooden shelter. As they dug the postholes, the holes filled with water. Next, the group retreated to the old hay barn at the north end of the property. But you couldn't build a fire on the floor beside the haymow. The group got permission to use the old wood stove in an abandoned house at the top of Plymouth Notch and to sleep in the adjacent barn. There they waited for the weather to clear. It didn't.

Two days before they had to start west again, they decided to head for Stratton Pond even in the rain. It was, after all, just drizzling that morning and it might be rained out. Right after breakfast the party set out for the Long Trail crossing on the Wardsboro-Arlington road, the back of the station wagon loaded with packs. By the time we reached the Long Trail crossing, the drizzle had developed into a heavy downpour. What to do? We were determined to have an overnight at a cabin we heard of on Stratton Pond, yet we knew that our last change of clothing, carefully saved for this expedition, would not stay dry under the simple ponchos we had.

"We can go barefooted and keep our shoes dry," somebody suggested.

"Yeah, then we'll have dry shoes to wear home, but no clothes."

"Well, there's nobody anywhere around this wilderness, certainly not in weather like this. Why don't we take all our clothes off, pack 'em in our rucksacks, and hike bare? It's warm enough."

The boys figured this was a swell way to solve the problem, and so it turned out. Hiking in the rain with freedom to splash and be splashed proved so popular that Timberlake has ever since enjoyed the Fifth Freedom, a freedom from clothes whenever no *rational* answer can be given to the question of why not?

The trail had gone through low places; it was now ankle deep in water; in several places it was even deeper. Some logging had been going on in the area, and through the steamy downpour we could hear loggers shouting at their horses. Because of the rain we never saw them. They too had evidently decided to ignore the rain, but probably not under such pleasant circumstances.

After slopping along the drowned trail for five miles, we came out in the early afternoon at the shack we had expected on the shores of Stratton Pond, then as now forest rimmed and unspoiled. We could see only a few feet out into the water, heavily pocked with raindrops, but it looked inviting.

"Let's dump our packs in the shelter and go for a swim?" someone suggested. "The water's great in a rain."

"Not me. I'm famished. Let's get the sandwiches out of the packs."

We opened the door of the shack. Inside, to our amazement, a young fellow lay on one of the double-decked wooden bunks. It turned out he was caretaker of the Stratton Shelter and the nearby Willard Ross Shelter. He stirred sleepily and sat up, rubbing his eyes. Our surprise couldn't have rivaled his as six boys and two men, all in their birthday suits, came pouring in. He recovered in time to welcome us properly; and in fact, started up a fire in the sheet-metal stove, offering us cocoa to wash down our lunch.

The boys dried off quickly in the heat, then sprawled out on the bunks after the meal, getting out the two blankets each had brought. Someone discovered the log book. We were fascinated by entries other hikers had left. We read them through and added our own remarks. Then we headed for the water. It *was* warm, sort of an extension of the soft, wet air. The rest of the day was sheer delight: in the water and out; then in to dry off and rest a bit; then out again. The caretaker told us of a raft a little way down the shore. The boys poled it over, and used it to dive from in deeper water.

Just as we started supper, a lone and bedraggled hiker showed up, a middle-aged man who was bent on hiking the Long Trail, come hell or high water. The high water *had* come, and it hadn't improved his shoes. The boys watched as he took from his heavy pack a small iron shoe stretcher and proceeded to put some new nails in the leather of the soles, which in the constant rain had separated into layers.

"Did — did it ever occur to you," one of the boys asked, "that your shoes would last better if you went barefooted?"

The withering glance the man shot at this boldness ended a promising dialogue.

After a final dip as the shadows deepened toward darkness the boys crowded into the snug cabin, dimly lighted by a lantern swinging from a rafter. A few minutes to dry off, and everyone was snuggled comfortably into his blankets, drifting off to sleep to the sound of the wood in the glowing stove.

It was a terrific trip, still remembered by the lucky hikers on probably the rainiest hike the Camp has ever taken. It set a pattern for all our hiking: rugged, venturesome, joyous and satisfying. The harder the trip the greater the thrill of achievement.

Later generations of Farm and Wilderness campers have gone off secure in the knowledge that their campcraft training is equal to any emergency. Their equipment has increased from the time of that memorable 1938 hike, but has still been kept to the minimum compatible with health and safety.

The trails have lengthened, too. A whole network fans out through the wilderness surrounding the Camps, first within the radius of the camp property, then to the "second circle," going on to shelters in the State Forest, or on the Long Trail, Vermont's "Footpath in the Wilderness." Besides these ready-made trails, the campers themselves, with the proper permissions, have blazed trails to distant outposts. Two of these have "halfway shelters" so that younger groups may set out after rest hour, spend the night at a trail shelter, and arrive at the outpost — and a good swim — by the following noon.

A third concentric circle of trails runs on to areas accessible only with transportation to a dropoff point, whence the hikers make their way back to camp during the following four or five days, bursting in with perfect timing and great éclat just as supper starts. Still other much-loved trips to prime hiking areas in neighboring states or to canoeing waters beyond our borders serve as challenge to the later years of a camper's experience. These, of course, require transportation both ways. A danger to the on-going trip program must be considered. Most of the unmarried staff will want to go on hikes. They can get so caught up in the lure of distant trails that the hikers of three or four years hence may be forgotten. These are the present nine- and ten-year-olds, the First Lodge. It is a crime for even these younger campers to miss the thrill of nights on the trail, sleeping under the stars, with a trail shelter handy in case of rain.

The needs of these young campers demand special attention. While their older brothers or sisters hike off with springy step, eyes fixed eagerly on a distant mountain, the nine- and ten-year-olds may explore some of the back trails of the camp property, always a rich adventure to such youngsters where the leadership is good.

The first week they return in time to spend a couple of hours preparing dinner at the cookout area near their cabins. Even their two cabin counselors cannot give these boys all the help they need these first weeks, so married staff and any other staff left in camp are invited to share in this important training. Perhaps a man or a woman may take only two youngsters as his charge. Together they will build their own small cooking fire, discussing meanwhile what makes a good site and what a dangerous one. Initially they may show these neophytes some of the mysteries of simple cooking, the kind of wood to use, the size of the fire (small), how much grease to use in frying, when to be alert to prevent something from boiling over, how to handle a kettle without danger to bare legs. But after the first demonstration a camper is on his own, unaware of watchful eyes in the background.

How else can one prevent those distressing pictures one sees in some camp booklets of a counselor bending over the fire while the kids stand around with their hands in their pockets?

In the cabins beyond the very youngest, the staff restraint in not taking over from clumsy hands need not be so great. There will be a nucleus of campers who have some degree of skill. Also, the effective learning of the Each-One-Teach-One type of instruction can be counted on. Old boys are glad to help the newcomers. The cabin counselors nevertheless cannot relax their covert watchfulness. It isn't easy to stand by while somebody spoils the soup or burns the beans; yet this is often the learning situation that prevents a young cook later on from tilting a whole meal into the embers.

Camps which are located in good hiking country need never lack for challenge to spark their hikes. Of course, it takes experience, enthusiasm, and imagination, but without reasonable amounts of these commodities one shouldn't be in camping in the first place. A little ingenuity can devise such variety in types of hikes that the same trails may offer endless allure. Above all, one must prevent hiking from turning into a competition for speed records. Campers should be ashamed of bragging that they "made the Diamond Trail over the Ridge in twenty minutes." Or rather their leaders should be ashamed of this distortion of values.

Just beyond the Catamount Clearing, and within earshot of where the old Bishop farmhouse stood, Timberlake boys and staff many years ago put up a long, low, brown-stained building called the Trading Post, repository for camping gear and hiking food. The Bishops would have difficulty understanding the ordered confusion in front of the Trading Post on a morning when hikes are starting out.

Here is the camp's big green truck, loaded with boys sitting on their gear, several shouting last-minute reminders to some pal in the crowd of onlookers not to forget to feed a favorite calf or a pen of chickens while they are hiking in from Brandon Gap or bushwhacking back to camp from Noys Pond. Two separate groups will be dropped off at different points. Beside the Trading Post stands a sleek station wagon with heavy-duty springs and a baggage rack. Hitched behind it is a trailer loaded with gleaming canoes. The boys beside the car wait impatiently for a pair to arrive with a box of frozen meat which will furnish their meal that night, before they go on the supplies which make up the bulk of the food for the trip.

With an ostentatious honking of its ancient horn, the open Packard shows up with a load of boys to be dropped off at Ulcer Gulch. From this drop-off point they will hike on into one of the outpost camps to finish a job on a dam. A battered jeep follows loaded with tools. This is a work crew determined to complete a log dam on the brook that runs through Chataugay.

While these ponderous trips wait to start, several jaunty groups file by, headed for the Diamond trail over the Ridge, or planning to climb the Juggernaut Trail into the Pico-Killington area. Neat packs ride high on bronzed shoulders. Several number ten cans swinging from wire handles give a certain music to their step. A group of younger boys heading for Tinker Gorge and two days at the Lower Shelter pass by. Their gaze is set toward the distant ridge; in their ears still ring the words of the Psalm they have heard that morning at Meeting for Worship. "He sendeth the springs into the valley, which run among the hills." The purpose of a hike may be that of improving a trail, or rerouting some section of it.

Under the inspiration of an avid signaler, the art of signaling — relaying messages in Morse code from hilltop to hilltop with a powerful flashlight — has become popular at Timberlake. Boys can be found at almost any free time conning their code book, or wigwagging with signal flags to friends. On a clear day a group with binoculars may be found on the sightly slope in front of the main lodge before a meal, straining to catch the wisecracks being flagged to them from some group at a pre-arranged lookout across the lake. Signaling is most fun when groups know the area well enough to deploy parties at a half-dozen high points in a line stretching off in one direction from camp. Then, if weather cooperates, a message can be relayed in from a distance of thirty miles away.

In the latter part of the summer, after considerable study of nature lore centering on edible plants of the area, two of the senior boys may be allowed to go off on a subsistence hike. They take with them nothing but shoes, shorts, a blanket and a knife for skinning some of the game they hope to snare. (From the Indian camp some such expeditions have made out successfully with even less equipment, just the traditional moccasins and bow and arrows of the Indian brave). The boys return famished from these trips but full of stories of the treasures of the wilds they have found.

Another group may take some section of the geodetic map and through running the trails in that area bring back a valuable map of the woods roads, trails, and streams.

Yet such special purposes, depending often on particular skills and interests, are not necessary to make a hike memorable. This is evidenced by the account turned in by a staff member who had taken out (with a junior counselor, of course) a group of eight thirteen-year-olds to visit a wilderness pond and return by a different route. So delighted were these youngsters with the wonders an alert imagination revealed that they voted to stay out an extra day.

"The first day we spent exploring the area around Little Rocky Pond. It yielded a large supply of blueberries for blueberry pancakes, also a number of good views. This was climaxed by a refreshing dip in the pond and a good meal. The following day the group navigated by compass and map cross country to another pond, passing the site of an old farm community and stopping to explore abandoned buildings and foundations and to speculate on their use. The pond itself was in part blocked by an elaborate system of beaver dams which made a fascinating study in elementary engineering.

"As the hike progressed we were able to get a heavy rope from another hiker we met and do some rock climbing over the spectacular White Rocks Cliffs; scramble through Clarendon Gorge, a chasm of rock and water; retrace sections of the Crown Point Military Road; watch the sun set from Beacon Hill and take a midmorning dip in yet another lake, Spring Lake, with the image of Killington reflected in the water around us.

"After voting to stay out an extra night we spent the last night on the top of Killington watching the view, the sunset, the tourists and later on a beautiful display of shooting stars. All of this plus the added challenge of feeding the trip in good style and learning to master three different types of wood stoves made the trip a memorable one for all concerned."

Trails blazed by the original Timberlake Farm and Wilderness Camp have led to other camps. Indian Brook, Timberlake's counterpart for girls, began three years after Timberlake. A group of older boys, based at a cabin on what is now the water front of the third camp, was the beginning of Tamarack Farm, the coed, teenage work camp. Some boys at Timberlake, despite all the hiking, could never get enough of wilderness. Thus began Saltash Mountain Camp, a small camp for forty boys which sets out to be really rugged. In camp, they go in for pioneer sports and games; logging is one of their activities; a Paul Bunyan Day tops their season. Cooking many of their own meals at outdoor kitchens near each cabin, the boys are nevertheless on the trail a good deal of the summer. There were boys who wanted to live even closer to nature. This resulted in Flying Cloud, a camp without any real buildings, but a set of beautiful twenty-foot tipis (and a shelter in which to store city clothes, and for what cooking is done centrally). It was the Indians who really knew how to cooperate with nature, and how to live comfortably in the wilderness. A whole new way of life, simple, rugged, satisfying, is challenging generations of boys who have lost the contact with the soil their forebears knew.

And still new vistas beckon. A favored outpost camping spot with a pond may well develop into a coeducational camp for younger children with a major interest in nature. Another "Indian" camp may develop for older boys, with a view to training leaders in a set of skills almost forgotten now.

Thus do the camps try to restore security to the youth of an urban generation — security and gaiety, as in their favorite hiking song:

> It's the far northland that's a-calling me away
> Where you see the loon and hear his plaintive wail,
> If you're thinking in your inner heart there's
>   swagger in my step,
> You've never been along the border trail.

This lilting song might well have been the refrain of a group of adolescents from Tamarack Farm as they swung along the trail across Killington in the early weeks of July one year. Down the line of staff and directors from previous generations, youngsters have been sold on the ideal of the simple life — and rugged. On a hike they need remarkably little to remain healthy and happy. To live in the wilderness one has to live simply. The gadgets on which one comes to depend cannot be taken along. They would be largely useless anyway. One begins to generate a certain pride in doing without; a pride also in improvising effectively.

A true spirit of camaraderie develops quickly under these conditions. Tricks of adaptation are passed along in a person-to-person situation which is very wholesome. Little wrinkles like scooping out a depression on the ground for one's hipbone under the bedroll; like finding the oily frayed bark of the birch tree for starting a wet-weather fire; like notching a hardwood sapling for hanging the pots over the embers — these are valuable bits of information humbly and gratefully received.

To judge from the cooking fire these teenagers from Tamarack have started in the fireplace before the trail shelter, much practice must have preceded this "practice" hike. The fire is neatly built, with a reserve of wood already cut and stacked under the overhanging eaves of the Adirondack shelter. Just for a change, the boys are bending over the fire, turning the hamburg patties, and the girls are dragging in the logs, sawing them up with a collapsible saw, then splitting them into manageable chunks. Competent enough generally, these girls are getting rattled by a barrage of commentary from the boys.

A word on these two members of the distaff set. They were Ellie Janson and Jane Long, two Indian Brook pals of the year before. Ellie is an old Indian Brooker, who started six years before in the Shining Waters cabin. But Jane came as a fourteen-year-old to Indian Brook, not an easy thing to do, particularly if you are handicapped by your early life. The first day at Indian Brook, for instance, when it came time for the first swim at the waterfront, Jane asked Ellie, her cabin mate, about the "facilities" at the waterfront. "Are there toilet articles in the cabanas?"

"In the *what?*" Ellie asked in unbelief.

"In the dressing cabins, where you get ready for the water; where you keep your bathing costume and all that."

With the adolescent pleasure in exaggeration and shock, Ellie replied carelessly, "Oh, you don't need to take *any*thing to the waterfront: just yourself."

"What do you mean?"

"Well, take off your shorts and halter and those shoes you've got on — and *go*, that's all."

"My God: you mean no bathing suit?"

"Well," Ellie hedged, "if it were early morning, or foggy, it wouldn't matter. Because of some stupid people who stop on the road way across the lake, we've had to wear suits more."

Ellie stuck by Jane during the early days of her introduction to the folk-ways of the Farm and Wilderness, for to somebody used to "cabanas" there was much to learn about simple living. Jane caught on fast, which was why the friendship grew. By the end of the season, Janie could flip a flapjack for a trail breakfast as skillfully as the rest. She had also forgotten about all her aches and pains, her sunburn, her bad back. Caught up in the excitement of trails in "the far Northland," she showed herself an able and adaptable member of any hiking group — contrary to the predictions of the interviewer who had visited with Janie before she was accepted for Camp. Even the two male cooks are having trouble finding anything to criticize in the girls' axmanship.

Just as this situation is beginning to get a little out of hand, and the last sleeping bags have been rolled out under protecting tarps against the onset of darkness, a file of strangers appears up the trail. The first boy discovers the expected shelter for the night is taken. He calls out in frank dismay to those behind him, and the unsettling news is echoed down the line.

A leader from the end of the line comes into view, and the counselor in charge of the Tamarack crew steps forward to meet him.

"Had supper yet?" he asks the stranger.

"No, we got started late," the leader offers apologetically. "How far is it to the next shelter?"

"Oh, some six or seven miles — isn't it, gang?"

"Too far." A tall youth has come up. "It's getting dark, and it's going to rain, any time."

"Look," offered one of the coed leaders. "We're all ready to eat. By the time you've settled your gear and got unpacked we can be out of your way, and you can have the fire. You won't have much time before darkness closes in."

The relief was so evident on the part of the newcomers as to make the first group sorry for them.

"How about it, gang," the leader proposed, after a huddle with several of his campers. "This is going to be a rainy night. Judging by the way these fellows are packed, they're not going to find it easy to set up for themselves in the woods. We can. Why don't we eat our hamburgs and then move out to that little plateau Jim and Dick camped on last year? 'Twon't take us long to move, and it's better we than they."

With grumbling from only a couple of members, the group bush-wacked farther up the mountain, setting up camp in a clearing from which in good weather one could get a view far down the slope. But this night it wasn't clear; in fact, by the time the last shelter was up, the upper side properly trenched for drainage, ground cloths spread, and sleeping bags rolled out, the rain had started. Nevertheless, the whole gang slept snug and dry through a long rainy night.

But Jane still lapsed at times back into the early patterns. She still took unnecessary gear with her on a trip. Just as the gang was packing the next morning she remembered that she had slipped a little case comb into a slot between two logs in the back part of the shelter. Ellie and she went down to retrieve it, figuring the group in the shelter would be up or even on their way by this time. The two girls were amazed to find the boys just getting up. The counselors had neglected to wake them, being themselves preoccupied with a futile attempt to start a fire in the rain. Unobtrusively, Ellie and Jane took over, showed the men where they could find some dry wood and left the fire well started, amid the admiring thanks of everyone.

All would have been fine, if the crew had let this little act of kind-ness go unadvertised. But the group from the coed camp were so pleased with themselves and with the flattering contrast they made with an un-trained group, that they composed a song about it on the way home. This song proved to be so funny (to the campers anyway) when it was pre-sented at the next council fire, that the director finally had to plead that it be turned off, since it was "fun at the expense of less fortunate people."

This excursion may epitomize the spirit of longer hikes and canoe trips. The packs on long trips are heavier; the camaraderie is deeper, since it has a number of days in which to grow, and the adventures are more varied — and some are spiced with danger. But the durability of man being what it is with the competent training these youngsters have had, they manage to solve their problems, avoid threatened dangers, and take hardships with a song. When they get back, everyone has grown in stature; everyone feels a warm glow of satisfaction at the way he has proved himself; they are knit together in a selfless bond which comes of sharing rigors and helping one another over hurdles.

A word about the camp encountered on that practice hike. It had obviously not discharged its duty to its campers. Leaders had let the hike go out lacking the preparation essential for comfort and safety under the conditions that specific hike might present. Such camps — fortunately their numbers are not large — not only damage all camping, but by failing to get the full measure of joy and experience for growth out of every hike, they short-change the campers and the parents who have trusted to their competence.

Organized camping is entering an era when its real potential and the crucial nature of its contributions are beginning to be discerned. The movement cannot afford to have parents find a single camp unable to produce what it claims it can. The benefits a camp states it gives, it must, in fact, give in full measure — with an added increment which cannot be put in words.

Camps, even the best of them, cannot instill in a child qualities he lacks completely, but they can bring out latent strengths; they can appeal to desirable character traits which perhaps because of circumstances have seemed to be sleeping.

But we must bring this long chapter to a close — and the hikes back into camp.

It's suppertime at Indian Brook. Raincoats and hats are hung all over the place. The steamy smell of damp wool indicates the mood of the weather outside, even before a girl looks up from her bowl of soup to exclaim, "Hey, look at that. It's just teeming out."

Presently the door opens, letting in a swirl of rain, also a file of girls in dripping raincoats and hats, each with a shoulder hump betokening a knapsack under raingear. Most of them are barefoot; all of them are dripping water on the floor. In the general brouhaha which ensues, the words of a gay song the newcomers are singing with more gusto than harmony rises above the confusion:

> Mud and nettles and smoke galore,
> Lovely and misty view;
> We hiked up Pico and wow, did it pour.
> Then Killington and the Long Trail too.

The grins and the rollicking measures get the message of this homemade effort across. The hikers are pleased as punch at their wilderness skills; they have exulted in this challenge and met it with swagger. Nobody can measure the strength, the self-confidence, and the habit of cheerful durability this trip has helped build into a new generation of American youth.

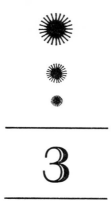

3

The bitter-sweet taste of labor

It's Friday night. In the camp lodge a square dance is in full swing. Girls in gay-colored flaring skirts; boys in khaki shorts and open shirts, with now and then a red bandanna at the neck or trailing out of a pocket, twinkle in and out of the intricate pattern of the dance. Eyes are sparkling, faces flushed with pleasure. The singing caller, one of the Camp's own counselors, turns toward the orchestra and gives them a signal. The tempo snaps up. Responding with shouts of pleasure to the quickened beat, the barefooted dancers accept the challenge, flying through the mazes of the Texas Star or Dip for the Oyster with never a false move. This is a midseason dance, when everybody knows the figures and each other. Dark faces here and there, both on the dance floor and in the orchestra, add variety and interest to the crowd.

The orchestra is having as much fun as the dancers. Fiddlers follow the beat of the pianist; perhaps a sax or a horn rises now and then above the rest; an accordion or two lumbers along, adding body and resonance to the music. The caller, knowing his group, suddenly shifts a command. Momentary confusion ensues, but the beat of the music and the sure rhythm straighten it out amid whoops of delighted laughter.

It is almost as much fun, visitors agree, to watch the dancers as to dance. Especially was this true when one could watch a couple like Sally Franz and Jack Fox. Sally was a cute number, and she knew it. It was evident that Jack Fox knew it, too. His blue eyes smiled on his partner when the pattern of the set brought the couple together again. He swung her with a vigor that swept her off her feet. Jack was big for his fourteen years; not in the least chunky, but just well filled out. From his light tousled hair to his sturdy legs and sinewy feet his frame bespoke action.

A normal, red-blooded, appealing teenager, you would say, wholesome and full of beans. You would be correct. What you wouldn't realize is that Jack Fox already had a police record. His parents had been advised to get him away from the gang which was taking over the upper middleclass suburb where the Foxes lived. The Fox parents were distraught. Having several years before moved from the city to what seemed country, they were dismayed to find themselves in Suburbia, with all the drawbacks of urban society.

"Jack's not a bad kid," his guidance counselor at the Cedarcroft Junior High had reassured Mrs. Fox. "His grades have been slipping, though the E.R.B. tests show that he has ability. He finds his extracurricular activities more absorbing than his studies. Recently, as you know, these pursuits have taken an—er—unfortunate turn. If it hadn't been for the understanding of the juvenile court—"

"I know," Mrs. Fox returned with a gesture of frustration. "Things can't go on this way. We thought we had given our children some values, but evidently they didn't stick. What do you suggest we do?"

"Have you ever thought of boarding school?"

"Why should we have to send our children to boarding school? We have a good home; we have fine standards; we—"

"But the values didn't stick, Mrs. Fox?" The counselor's voice was polite, his gaze quite impersonal.

This was how it happened that Jack got shipped off to summer camp. The Foxes didn't actually have to crate Jack up and send him off by force; the boy had been at a camp several years before. But now it was kid stuff, and Jack took a dim view of it.

For some time his letters were scrawled in pencil and under evident duress. "No lettee no eatee" was the Sunday evening rule at the Camp. After the first Sunday evening, when Jack discovered that they meant it, the boy didn't miss having his supper ticket ready as the bread line jostled its way beside the serving counter in the camp kitchen to pick up the makings of the Sunday picnic supper.

"What a lousy camp," Jack's first effort read. "They make you do a lot of dumb things like sawing up logs for the paths. The other day I forgot to turn my tag on the tag board and got docked."

"Almost got hooked on this letter," the next epistle began. "Gordie, that's the Lumberjack counselor, decided to collect the letters early. I was busy, and didn't get it done. So — here 'tis."

The Fox parents could only conjecture as to what Jack was "busy" with.

The next letter began to show an interesting cryptology. "I passed my bowman for Pioneers, but Rich — he's head of campcraft — won't let me try my rapelling on Spruce Ledges. Says I'm too cocky. What a square."

Then letters began to appear in between the No Lettee No Eatee ones, as for instance the air-mail special-delivery missive explaining that you had to have parental permission "and all that garbage" for a subsistence hike on which older boys would go off in pairs with nothing but a sheath knife and a blanket. This was for later in the season, but a letter from home was the first step.

There followed some time later a jubilant note telling of a steak roast to be tendered the boys in Jack's cabin in recognition of their cleaning up a soggy mass of rotting foundation logs where an ancient spring tank had been mouldering away, part of a water system no longer used. The feast seemed not so much in celebration of completing a grubby job as to note the fact that the boys had used some imagination. They had decided to dig out a pool on the erstwhile site, to catch the now useless overflow from the spring. Then they had set in hemlock seedlings and other shade-tolerant flora to landscape the pool.

"And it was all my idea," Jack added modestly.

But after that, the letters began to skip entirely. The boys were off on long hikes and a canoe trip, one hastily written card reported from a way station.

To understand something of what had been going on in the mind of Jack Fox, it would be well to look in on the Lumberjacks, and to meet their counselor, Gordon Brown, as well as Gordie's junior assistant, Tim Lincoln. Named like all the senior lodge cabins for wilderness callings — the others were the Rivermen, the Trappers, Foresters, and Rangers —

the Lumberjack's cabin was an old slabsided structure on the wooded shore between the water front and Paradise Island which marked the entrance to the Timberlake Cove from the main body of the Lake. The waves down in front of the cabin lapped a rickety construction known by courtesy at the Lumberjack Dock. Homemade, obviously, and as surely aging under the racking pressures of winter ice and summer use. When you ran out on it for a dive you had to be really quick or the shaky structure would throw you before you could make the jump in proper form.

The cabin, like the dock, looked back on many summers, and on many groups of boisterous, rough-and-ready, warmhearted, argumentative, fun-loving, gay and serious, boyish and mature fourteen-year-olds like the present one. Besides Jack Fox, there was Jimmy Winters, who bragged about the five years he'd been at Timberlake, a tough character from Brooklyn, but a good egg. There were Steve Goldberg, Frankie Ray and his pal Gerry Enders, black boys from Birmingham. Tim Jeffers was the quiet type — mousy, Jack thought at first, a runt who could be brushed off with one sweep of his paw, but Jack had come to accord a good bit of respect to this wiry youngster from Ohio. Then there were Vic Anderson, fat, the cabin loud-mouth, and Jim Read, who never said enough for you to figure *what* he was. Gordie Brown, counselor par excellence, was an all-right guy. He could take on the boys, three or four at a time, in a rough up, and brush them off gently, like flies. But this was only once: most of the time Gordie governed by a nod, or a smile, or — not too often — a frown. He was a guy who had been a teenager himself. He knew the ropes all right and you couldn't shock him. But what he had to say was good medicine, after you stopped to think it over. He had had more than one talk with Jack during that rocky first week. His keen blue eyes looked right through you. Nothing could stay hidden. He laid the cards on the table, straight out, so you could see everything; and what he said hit home. Jack had never felt so like crawling down a crack as when Gordie began holding the boy up to see himself; yet he left you feeling good too, after a while, and knowing that he trusted you to wise up before you did anything really dumb.

Gordie seemed to think a lot of his junior counselor, Tim Lincoln, Link for short, to distinguish him from Tim Jeffers. Link was from Wilburforce. Sometimes he "talked big," all about Black Power and what it was going to do to this country. But Link wasn't able to make this sort of talk sound alarming. He was too friendly and understanding to make the Black Power menace seem for real. And the muscles under that ebony skin were as hard as nails. Link never allowed himself to get into a brawl with the boys, like Gordie, but everyone had a healthy respect for his strength, increasing all the time, he said, because of the set of bar bells he worked out with regularly in front of the cabin. Link said the Lumberjacks were a great bunch of boys; Gordie agreed they'd do all right; only seven or eight of them needed shaping up.

Jack found it wasn't so much sports through which you were expected to shape up, but more through work, believe it or not. They had real work here, stuff like chopping down big trees in the woods, then barking them, sawing them into lengths, creosoting them, and setting them in as risers in the endless paths down the steep slopes throughout camp. When other work gave out, if it ever did, there were always gullies down the mountainside called paths, and they needed immediate aid to stop erosion, or, as Gordie remarked, the hillside would someday dissolve and flow away. The first few days Jack couldn't care less whether it did or not; then somehow the place began to get under his skin. The old boys loved their camp; Gordie did, too, quite obviously, though he didn't talk about it directly. Gradually Jack began to pick up a bit of this attitude.

It was the beginning of this new feeling that made him accept the first weekly stints in the camp garden without much griping; and besides, he didn't want to let Gordie down.

The Timberlake garden amazed Jack as he followed the file of boys climbing up the steep path which skirted the Timberlake Farm. A strip of rich brown soil five hundred feet long, and many rows wide, lay steaming in the sun. This tillage was surrounded by a ten-foot deer fence, through which you could get glimpses of the ridge behind the garden and the wooded slopes across the lake, with mountains beyond.

But there wasn't much time at first to look at mountains. Jack found himself with a hoe in his hand listening to a lecture by Abe Linn, the gardens counselor, on how to use a scuff hoe to build a dust mulch in the corn rows before the stalks were high enough to provide their own shade. Sometimes you had to get out patches of weeds between the rows. Then you had to hill up the stalks against the sudden thunderstorms that raced down from the mountain. In hilling you had to be careful not to dig deep, else you might cut some of the roots of the plants and weaken them. You had to get out any weeds left between the hills, and even thin the hills if there were more than three stalks. But this was tricky, too, for you had to be careful not to loosen the root system of the other stalks.

Jack thought he knew all about hoeing. He'd never done any, but then, any moron could swing a hoe. All you had to do — "Hey, you, over there!" The gardens counselor was calling to *him*. Now he strode over to Jack. He was a Taiwanese, but master of enough English to be very explicit!

"Say, man, where'd you learn to hoe?" Abe asked, with a twinkle in his eye that took the sting away. "Now watch me again. You are hoeing *back* on yourself, see? And covering up some of the weeds you want to slice out with the edge of the hoe. Then you can't see to get the next bunch. They'll be partly covered up. Always go forward, never back on yourself. Let's see you try it."

With a bit less self-assurance Jack took the proffered tool. The counselor stood beside the boy for a moment.

"Don't worry about not understanding the first time I told you. Lots of counselors, even, who come up here with their cabins, hoe backwards, or try to. You can't, in tough going. When you strike some of that witch grass at the end of the garden up there you'll be glad to know the right technique."

The witch grass-deal came the next week, in fact. It was still early in the season and the garden crews were still pretty much made up of cabin groups. The morning was hot. That was the time to get after witch grass, Abe Linn confided to the Lumberjacks as they sat on the edge of the tillage to get their briefing for the morning.

"The soil is dry, and you can pull out the roots a lot easier than when they have wet soil to cling to."

The man showed the Lumberjacks where the crew of the day before had left off. "Only eight rows here, and not over thirty feet long. If each of you does a row, you'll have this whole corner of the garden cleaned up by swim time, and it will look like a million dollars."

Huh! Big deal. Looked more like a real mess and fully forty feet long, not thirty. The guy must be nearsighted.

But the others dug in. Even Link Lincoln, who had come up with the Lumberjacks, was taking this seriously. Jack remembered the bit about always hoeing forward. It did make things easier; he began to get the rhythm of the hoe. The sun felt good on his arms and back; his bare feet liked the feel of the warm soft earth. There was a constant banter of comrades side by side, straddling rows and chopping manfully at the enemy. Link started one of his freedom songs, and the boys took it up, keeping time with the chop-chop of the hoes.

As the morning heated up, the singing stopped. The octet began to stretch out unevenly, some ahead on their rows, others starting to lag behind. Vic Anderson set out for the far end of the garden, explaining that he needed to get a drink of water. He was gone a long time. Then Larry Summers and Steve Goldberg put down their hoes, started for the spigot.

"Listen, fellahs," Link called to them. "We don't wanna leave this piece unfinished. Linn says to the Trappers or the Rangers when they come up, he say, 'First go over there and finish up that piece the Lumberjacks left yesterday.' We don't want that."

The boys were back promptly. Jack began to wonder was he getting too much burn on his fanny. Most of the boys had stripped off their shorts when they came up, knowing this sequestered spot, like the water front, was a good place to get rid of the telltale band. Everybody seemed to covet what was tooted as "the onlee all-over tan — without the telltale band, a Timberlake tan."

Jack went over to get his shorts from where he had stuffed them in one of the rectangles of the fence. As he drew them on, he heard a distressed bleat from below in the TL Farm. He peered through the fence, trying to see down through the brush to the calf pasture. Yes, it was Hercules. Some dumb cluck had tied that bull calf's tether too short, and the dimwitted animal had wound himself up in his chain. There he was steaming in the sun, calling for help. Jack strode swiftly along the fence to the gate going into the garden. He approached the animal, who stood passively surveying his rescuer.

"I oughtn't to help you out," Jack remarked to Hercules, "not after the way you treated me the other day. I'm not taking any chances with you again, dragging me all over the cow turds by that silly chain of yours."

He inspected the chain, decided it was too complicated to get it unwound. Besides, Hercules had chewed off all the grass in that spot: he'd have to be moved. That presented another problem. If he pulled up the iron bar, could he get it into the stony ground without something to pound with? He looked around for a stone.

"I don't trust you," he shot at the animal. "Soon's I get the crowbar out, you'll probably try to bolt." He went on down to the little barn to get a sledge hammer.

By the time he returned to the garden, the gang had passed him by. Even Vic Anderson, already slimming down, was well beyond him.

"Have a nice siesta beside the faucet?" Vic asked innocently. Jack thought of explaining, then fell to chopping viciously instead.

All had finished but Jack when the swim bell rang. One by one they came down from the raspberry patch along the upper side of the garden, munching handfuls of the luscious berries. They scattered to pick up clothing left along the rows. A couple of the boys swung over to where Jack was working and made half-hearted offers to help.

Link strode over, Abe Linn was nowhere to be seen.

"Tim Jeffers and a couple of boys offered to finish your row before going up for berries," he confided, "but I knew you'd want to get it done yourself. What happened?"

Jack told him briefly.

"Well, I'm glad that was it," he replied. "You can finish before lunch if you keep at it." He turned and set out after the Lumberjacks.

All alone Jack kept on till the sun stood directly above him. He had already missed swim, but his row was nearly done. Only ten feet more.

Suddenly he felt very hungry; then he felt faint. The heat steamed up from the ground in waves, swirled around him until he thought he would have to sit down. He looked grimly to the end of the row, wiped a drop of sweat from the end of his nose with the back of a dirt-streaked arm. This was some different from working with a crowd of fellows you like, with enough wisecracks going back and forth to make the time speed by, and with the fun of matching your work against the output of the next man. Perhaps he *should* stop. He could explain to the gang about the calf and all that.

"Never make excuses," he remembered Gordie saying once as the cabin was getting ready for bed. "Your enemies won't believe them and your friends don't need them."

The lone Lumberjack had time to heed various sensations which never seemed to appear when the crowd was around. His back ached, his head throbbed, and his shoulders hurt. The sun was blazing hot. He began to think of sunstroke. He was honest enough to decide the idea was not likely.

Though he had kept doggedly at the job when he was learning the crawl, a water front counselor was there to encourage him. This was different. He bent again to his work. He had come into an area of thicker grass, so that he found himself alternately chopping at the tenacious stuff with the edge of his hoe and going down on his hands and knees to pull out the roots.

Occasionally he allowed himself to look on to the end of the row and assess the amount left to do. When he got it to an estimated five feet he began to take heart. But also the sun was hotter and he was more bushed. Finally there were only three feet left to go — but those three feet were solid witch grass. Three feet, at *last!* He *would* finish if it killed him. He stood up a moment, threw his shoulders back. The sun was a torment, and one damned horsefly. Two feet. The last two feet are the hardest, the hardest. Just two feet — no, not *quite* now. Chewing down to a foot, but this was all witch grass. He chopped at some of it viciously with his hoe. Wow! Too tired. He'd pull roots a while. He flopped down on his knees again. The sweat trickled down his back. Only a foot to go. Come on, now, let's see this thing through. Give it the gun. Let's get that last foot. And no sloughing off. If he died doing it, he was going to do it right. His last act. They'd find him keeled over at the end of the row. But he was a boy who put it through. When he saw his duty, he done it — no, *did* it, Gordie would say, viewing the body. His face must be crusted with mud from slapping at that fly with his dirty hand. Hey! Only one little square left now, and pull, pull, chop, chop. *That was done!* The whole blasted row done, done, *done.* With an effort he straightened up to survey his work.

"Not a weed left," he remarked aloud. "And the sides are just as smooth as anybody's. Gollies, that looks keen."

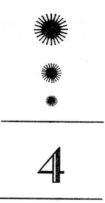

4

Footsteps up a mountain

The early morning sun shining through a cleft in the hemlocks that topped the eastern ridge above the garden painted the grass of the Catamount Clearing with brighter emerald. Dewdrops on the grass blades sparkled like diamonds. The tangle of tawny day lilies that edged the Clearing had survived from the days of the old Bishop farmhouse which stood on almost the same spot.

The Clearing was backed by a heavy framework from which hung a great iron ring, an old locomotive tire from the erstwhile Rutland Railroad. The sun's rays played over the sturdy form of a tall boy from the Rangers' cabin standing with feet apart and sledge hammer poised, awaiting the signal to strike the gong. Half a dozen cronies stood waiting also, watching for the arrival of the counselor who was host for the day and would give the word for the Meeting for Worship bell.

"OK, Long-Hair—if you can see to ring."

The counselor, clipboard under one arm, grinned as he appeared up a path from the direction of the waterfront. The Ranger swung his sledge with ponderous rhythm, the muscles of his arms and shoulders standing out distinctly as he wielded the heavy hammer. His black hair flopped down over his eyes. An even dozen deliberate strokes, and the boy cradled the sledge in the ring, still vibrating from the blows. He fell in step with his cabin mates as they headed up the dusty road toward the woods where the Meeting for Worship was held. These were the Rangers, the oldest group in camp, a group charged with setting a good example for the others. They had extra privileges, such as ringing the Meeting for Worship bell and the swim bells; but they also had responsibilities, as they discovered.

Other boys, singly and in pairs and groups, appeared from various paths and fell in with the Rangers; this senior group turned up a broad pathway which started in front of the long brown building which had once been the center of camp. Anyone standing on the broad veranda of the lower lodge and watching closely the groups as they started up the path through the stand of maple and yellow birch could get a view of the whole camp as it filed by, both boys and staff.

Here was a little towheaded youngster with blue eyes and narrow, sensitive face. A shy boy, he walked alone. Behind him two boys, probably cabin pals, trudged along cheerfully, like a couple of puppy dogs trotting ahead of their master. Probably the master was the tall youth with the loose-jointed, swinging gait bespeaking relaxation and patience, virtues needful for easy living with the tender ages of his charges. They would be the Wigwam, the nine-year-olds.

Several Big Lodgers followed, one a dreamy-eyed individual with long tapering fingers which could caress a violin. His absent glance saw little of what it fell upon. Walking behind him was a tense, slender youngster, with glasses and a great shock of unruly hair. A budding scientist, perhaps. The next boy, walking with the confident step of a person at peace with himself, was stocky and well-built. He would be an easygoing comrade, probably full of bubbling fun. He felt no need to join up with somebody for security. The next pair of jokers understood each other completely, as evidenced by the almost wordless banter they kept up as they hiked along.

About the man who followed, a counselor in his late twenties, there was something of a studious air heightened by the scholar's steel-rimmed glasses. Nothing in his appearance suggested the quiet strength which made him the idol of the whole cluster of Big Lodgers who trooped along behind him.

The path wound its way to a cleared area in the woods, an area of rustic benches built in concentric squares, with no real "facing bench." But traditionally, the longest bench on the far side had become the facing bench. Here sat anyone who felt a responsibility for the Meeting. A cabin group who had asked to present some thought at the Meeting would take this seat.

The boys poured quietly into this area from the path in a steady stream, taking seats as they wished. Usually, cabin groups sat together, following a favorite counselor in order to sit with him.

When the last stragglers had arrived, a hush fell over the group. Heads bowed in silent meditation, or stared straight ahead at the ancient sugar maples in the woods beyond, or watched the mist lifting on the mountain across the valley. Many of the boys here had no previous experience with Quaker worship or any worship, perhaps. But gradually its healing quiet stole over them; they have grown to cherish these precious minutes set aside from the routine of the day.

After a few minutes of silence, generally somebody will speak, sharing simply some thought he has been pondering. Otherwise, what goes on in the boys' minds during the Meeting is no doubt as varied as their individual needs, their ages, their temperament. Perhaps some are little touched by the magic of these few moments of silence; some use the time to think over events of the recent past.

—Funny thing, that guy Mansfield spilling the soup last night, Jees, did I laf. But he had a mess to clean up, poor kid. I shoulduv helped him.

—Three, four, five, six — six times somebody's slapped a no-see-um. Glad they chew up other people. Andy says a few more days and they'll be gone.

I *can* get that stroke. It's not so tricky. I almost had it yesterday. Gotta get it today.

—Fooey. This stuff's for the birds. I want outa here. Need to get the game started. Only one morning for Senior Lodge sports. I'll get the Cabin Reps to bring it up this Sat'dy.

—What was that new counselor reciting the other morning? Some poem about a flower in a wall. "If I could understand what you are —" Something like that. "I should know what man and God is." How could that tell what God is? Well, those big maples, that warbler. Wonder what kind it is? Hafta ask John Rip if he heard it. 'Way off, like that. Kinda mysterious. Wonder if it's like the voice they say speaks to you when you're real quiet.

—If my feet were cut up the way Jake's are, I'd put shoes on for a while, 'stead of drawing pictures in the dust with my big toe.

—Damn that Jake Markly, laffing when I slipped in the cow turd with that calf. I'd like to rub his ugly mug in it. Oh well, so what! S'pose I'd a laffed too. Jake's not a bad egg. Wonder how his counselor missed making him put shoes on.

—That banty hen didn't have any water when I came along yesterday. Lucky I stopped up there to check. Her chicks were thirsty as anything. You could see how happy they were to have some clean water. Bill shoulda put it up on a little block of wood the way Clayton showed him. Then the mother hen wouldn't scratch their dish full of leaves. Those ducklings sure are growing. They're so hungry when I feed them. And they know me now. I mustn't forget them again like the other day. Eben was sore.

—Cripes, won't this thing ever end? Would be our only morning for a game. Next week we'll be off on hikes.

—What *am* I searching for? What am I? Is there what that fella called a soul, or is it just me thinking. But what's "me"? And what's God? How could there be a God? How could there not be? How could it just happen? Like that box they spoke of, and shaking a lot of dust in it. Couldn't ever jump into a pattern, just by chance. Not in a million years, or a million million. That's harder to believe than there's a God. But what's He like; or what's it like? Must be everywhere, in everything. Must be, if He's at all.

—That Maynard kid. I'll have to get time to talk with him. Full of hostility; and scared. Else he wouldn't act that way. Wonder what gives at home. Here's one kid that needs help. Well, here goes the next free evening with Frieda. But no other time. She'd want me to, else I wouldn't love her so. God, she's pretty.

—I've got the guys to lay off that Gordon kid; I think I have. And I started that last one, myself. He can't help the way he is, poor guy. Maybe I'm not all that perfect.

—Sure was great the other night when Charlotte slipped out of the square dance between numbers and I followed her. Wonder if she figured I would. Guess so, or why did she duck into the mail room. She

knew what she wanted. Guess I could've given it to her. She wanted me
to feel her legs—'way up. Hell, is there any reason we shouldn't? I know
Curt says even the Pill won't make it sure. But his other reasons, like
waiting, everything in its time, the things you might spoil if you don't
hold off for a few years. I wonder. Hafta ask him more about that.

—That mist on the mountain. Gone now, just while we've been sitting
here. Why does the ridge seem so beautiful? What *makes* me think it's
beautiful? Is that God? Must be: no "survival value" in a thing like that.

Dear God—if there is a God! Anyway, dear God, I sure need help.
Help me not to act so mean, and say such mean things. I gotta stop
thinking them; that's where it starts. That was what Bob meant when he
talked to me the other day. Help me to —

Somebody was speaking. So quietly had he begun that it was a moment before everybody started listening. It was a twelve-year-old, a Big
Lodger, a new boy, and still shy. But something had impelled him to
share an idea, and there he stood, a wool shirt tied around his middle by
the sleeves. He gathered courage as he spoke.

"That kid that stopped in here yesterday. His father's the vet. that
came in to check on Tinker Bell and her calf. He's bin here before. We
were all lying there in the sun by the water front, a whole bunch of us,
and he looked lost. He asked us didn't we feel ashamed, all bare like
that. Then he said something that set me thinking. Said his dad had told
him we didn't ever get into fights or use sharp words to each other, even.
Well that's not true, of course. His dad didn't happen around at the
right time. But I've noticed it myself. We don't snap at each other here,
the way kids do at home. Maybe you think you don't like some guy.
Maybe you get mad at him. Then you figure p'raps he's just having
trouble, inside, and—Oh, I can't explain it. But you get over being mad."

A long speech for a boy. He sat down, embarrassed, but probably
also satisfied that he had managed to give voice to something that needed
expression.

A few moments of silence. Then one of the Rangers stood up.

"Come to think of it, there *is* less yakking at each other than at
school. I'm sure we do like each other, well, pretty much, and most of the
time. But we all have our moments. I know when I get mad at some guy,
then I start thinking how he got the feeling that makes him so offbeat.
Mostly I didn't used to do this at home. Maybe it's something here;

maybe it's this Meeting every day. It doesn't keep me from saying the wrong thing, but it does make me feel rotten about it afterwards. So perhaps it *is* good. I know for instance, when we turned in here I wanted to get down to the field for that game instead, but maybe this is important too."

A counselor was speaking: "I think it's like what Rusty was saying in Meeting the other day. He used a big word, empathy, which means you try to put yourself inside the guy that's bugging you and try to feel what it looks like inside him, and looking out through his eyes with the things he may have to live with and fight down. By the time you begin to figure this out, you don't want to hurt him, or if you have, you try to make it up. Maybe later on you can give him a little push the way it would be better for him to go."

There was silence again. For a while nobody wiggled, no one slapped at the bugs, nobody drew pictures in the dirt with his toe. A depth of silence that was creative came over the group. Then one of the older counselors turned to his neighbor and extended his hand in the handshake that, repeated down the group, "broke" the Meeting to end it. Not a few participants as they shook hands with a neighbor smiled into his eyes with a deeper understanding.

It isn't every day—or some years not even every week—that campers speak. Sometimes staff or director seem to carry the whole responsibility. But if such a gathering, where only a few are Quakers and used to a silent meeting, has managed to establish an atmosphere of humble searching together, of honesty and compassion, the cumulative effect through a whole season can be considerable in promoting a general feeling of friendliness and good will through the camp. If besides this, the camp is at some pains to set up relationships based on cooperation rather than the competition which is so much a part of life, then visitors will remark on the lack of disputes that reach the shouting stage or result in fights.

Over the thirty-five years that Timberlake has operated, a definite change in attitudes in the Meeting is evident. Three decades ago there was much interest in reading a passage from the New Testament, then trying to interpret it and apply it to everyday life. Now we deal with a generation of boys, and staff, who for the most part know nothing about the Bible, and care less. The old forms, the terminology, have passed away.

It may be just as well. The present generation, often deeply committed to social change, dreaming of a just society, a more compassionate nation, has too often found their elders mouthing religious texts while condoning flagrant injustice. The danger, of course, is that of pouring out the baby with the bath water, of rejecting all religious truth because of its association with "hypocrites" quoting scripture.

But the yearning remains, the shining idealism, the groping for understanding of reality, the lurking suspicion that the mechanistic philosophy of the day is too simple, too pat to fit all they see.

It is a more honest, more socially concerned generation that staffs our camps now. Such men and women may be impatient of the old forms, but they think nothing of spending themselves without stint on some youngster who needs understanding. And they bring a degree of observant sensitivity to the task which could not be surpassed by the staffs of an earlier generation.

*   *   *

The water front, that relaxed social center of the Camp on a hot afternoon, offers many shrewd insights to a perceptive counselor into the reasons behind boyish behavior. A counselor who is himself at peace will seize the opportunity of a teachable moment.

He will notice the boy who sits by himself looking moodily out at the raft and the few brown figures still cavorting around on it. The boy had sat alone the day before, the counselor remembered.

Easing himself down beside the youngster, the man remarked that a bad toe could sure wreck a fellow's swimming. The boy didn't even bother to inspect the staff toe. This was something out of the ordinary, for with a group that usually went barefooted, the various types of stubbed toes were always a matter of interest. There was silence.

"Quite a game of Follow-the-Leader out there by the rafts. Did you get in it?"

The boy shook his head.

The counselor smiled. "Dumb of me to ask that: I could have looked at your hair. You haven't been in this afternoon. Why not, on a day like this?"

"Guess I don't care that much about swimming."

"Didn't I see you in that game of water polo the other day. No?"

"Not me." The first flicker of a smile. "I got mine early in the season."

"Whaddayuh mean, you got yours? Ducked, or something?"

The boy turned to look at the counselor, as if to decide whether it was worth going into details. The frank eyes and the friendly smile were reassuring.

"Well, it wasn't anybody's fault. I got into a hassle by the goal there. Five or six guys, Rangers, most of them, trying to get the ball. Somehow I got shouldered under, and then a couple of feet pushed me down. They didn't even know I was there, I guess; too excited. But I didn't have much air with me when I went down, and I got kind of scared."

"That can be bad, when you need out and can't figure which way is up. Everything above you seems to be full of bodies. Didn't ship any water, did you?"

"Well, some, I got out and kind of choked a little. That junior counselor over there was real nice. He came over and asked me if I was all right. I told him I was and he went away."

"And since then you haven't been swimming."

"Oh yes, I like to swim. I just still remember that time, and I keep away from any gang like that."

"Well, you're a bit light for some of those Senior Lodgers." The counselor inspected the trim form. "You'll be taking on some meat pretty soon, I'd say."

The boy tossed his head slightly, as if this were not a favorite subject.

"But you've got a good frame for the crawl. Slender, and good shoulders. Do you do the crawl?"

A momentary gleam came into the boy's gray eyes. "I've been trying to get it," he confided.

"Well, keep at it. It's great when you finally have it. Smooth, and fast. Wow! What else have you been doing?"

"I've almost got my woodsman's rating. Just have to get out on a practice hike. And I *was* writing for the News."

"You haven't kept it up?"

The boy shook his head.

"Why not?"

"Oh, I dunno. Don't seem to be able to write the way they want."

"How come, 'the way they want'? Is there a formula?"

"Well, not exactly, I guess. But the Board—that's some of the guys—have been there a long time. They get everybody together each Monday and talk about what's needed for that week's issue. You probably know that. Then different guys speak up and say they'll write such and such a piece. Coupla times I spoke up, but somebody got in before me. So I just wrote up my own piece and handed it in. Never heard from it."

"But you like to write?"

"Oh, so-so. I guess you'd say yes. 'Bout the way I like to draw."

"You draw, too, do you?"

"Well, I like to make pictures. Sometimes they go with what I'm writing, and sort of explain it where I can't say it in words."

"Say, you might be valuable. Guy who can illustrate his own stories. Does the Board know you sketch?"

"I don't guess so. They never asked me. Why should they?"

"Well, no use hiding your light under a bushel. Ever try handing in a feature article, something that struck you as interesting about the camp? Your first year here, isn't it?"

The boy nodded. "What about an article on the new porcupine at the nature center? You could draw a picture of Porky climbing that tree they stuck in his cage. Be real neat, don't you think?"

The boy picked up a twig from the grass, held it in his hand as if weighing the idea. "I might try it. Naw, I guess not. The editor comes from my cabin, and he doesn't like me."

"Whaddayuh mean he doesn't like you? Why should he dislike you?"

"None of the kids in the cabin like me." This was stated in a matter-of-fact way, as if the boy were saying, "My cabin has eight boys, and two counselors."

There was silence, while the counselor picked a blade of grass and tried to blow on it.

"Must be the wrong kind of grass," he offered. "When I was a kid we used to take a good broad blade and you could sure make a noise with it. Ever try? — That's not normal, you know, all the kids in a cabin down on one fellow. Any idea why?"

"Well—Maybe I've made sarcastic remarks a couple times."

"That does it, quick. Would you like to have them like you?"

"Why not? But it's done now."

The counselor turned to look his young charge full in the face.

"Listen, man. It's never done. You can always change a thing like that. Boys forget quickly. Give them another type of behavior, and they'll dig the new type just as fast. Want to know how?"

The boy was listening.

"Well, here's a formula. I've seen it work. First, when you feel like saying something mean, you swallow it instead. You can do that, you're a good observer. Somebody probably comes late to straighten up his gear under the bunk. You set it in order for him. He'll remember that. And somebody else would like the cabin representative to ask at the Cabin Council for more free evenings. If you feel this way, talk with the guy about it, and let him know you'll stand with him to get this over to the Representative. Lots of little things, if you start noticing. You can change the whole thing in a week. Try it and see."

The first gong for dinner had rung. The crowd, except for a few avid sun bathers, had taken off for their cabins or started up the steep path to the dining hall.

"Well, we're going to be late if we don't start soon. But try it, will you?"

The boy nodded his head, the first positive reaction the man had had from him.

"And look, fellah, why don't you try that piece on the zoo, or some other bit you've noticed around here. Know that sign up on the ridge, where the trails cross—'Danger, Piliated Woodpecker Crossing'? Get some of the dope on those birds—they're rare, you know—and do a little feature on a piliated woodpecker. I'll bet you'll find yourself on the Board before the end of camp. Feature Editor, you know. Will you do it?"

The boy got up. For just a moment his eyes met his counselor's. "Yuh. Thanks, I'll give it a try."

"Good. And don't forget the cabin deal, either. Interesting thing. Give it a week. I'll see you later."

After dinner, when the counselor could catch the boy's cabin leader without being seen, he asked about the boy.

"Oh, Ted Lampson? Yes, he's been moping for a week now. Started when he got a letter from home, his mother, I suppose. Then yesterday he had another. I found him crying in his bunk. Not usual for a kid that age to cry. So I wormed it out of him. His folks are planning a divorce. He worships his father, but I suspect his mother has been disillusioning the poor kid and now he doesn't know what to think."

"Yuh, that can do it. Not for me to judge, but —. Well, see if you can follow up on that suggestion about the *News,* that is, if you think it's good."

"Sure it's good. I shoulda thought of it myself. He's a natural for that weekly. Likes to use words. That's part of the trouble in the cabin. He's too flip with a remark that hits home."

Some time later, when the boys got the new issue of *Camp News,* there was a full-page feature story titled, "How We Almost Got Chocolate Milk." There was a picture in one corner at the top showing a bunch of boys all upending milk bottles and rubbing their stomachs appreciatively. The byline carried the name of the lonely boy on the water front. The text read in part:

Most schools have some sort of student council, but it doesn't work. The kids all know the faculty adviser is told by the principal what he wants done and not done. But if we want something—even if just a couple of boys want it—they can team up and ask their Cabin Representative to bring it up at Cabin Meeting. That is, providing other boys in the cabin go along with the idea.

Last week two of us started a campaign to get chocolate milk instead of ordinary milk. The rest of the cabin didn't care either way, so the Representative took it to the Council. The Council thought it was "O.K." So the Chairman of the Cabin Representatives brought it up at the Camp powwow last Saturday night. Should we have chocolate milk or shouldn't we? What'll it be?

"Chocolate milk," 'most everybody shouted. "We want chocolate milk."

But then somebody shouted, "Do we have to have it even if we don't like it?" some others chimed in.

So we agreed that we'd ask to have both. The Secretary of the Cabin Council—that's Joe Blum—was told to see Al about getting it.

Somebody was nice enough to ask the director if he thought it was a good idea. "It's all right by me," he said. "See if Al can get it."

So Joe went to Al in the kitchen.

"What, get chocolate milk?" he asked. "Isn't my business

complicated enough, getting meals for 120 hungry boys, always hungry, and my meals hard to figure how much of each and then no matter how you figure you got some left over?"

So we don't have chocolate milk. And it's easy to see who runs the Camp. Not the director. Not the counselors. Not the Camp powwow. It's Al. But he sure knows how to cook.

Another boy was climbing his mountain. The article was one of the footsteps. Smaller steps in the Meeting for Worship undoubtedly preceded it.

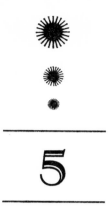

5

Education can be fun

An ancient Latin precept bearing on the education of boys states that boys up to twelve should never be required to master anything they must learn sitting down. Considering that our sedentary culture has gone to the other extreme with its harvest of middle-aged heart attacks, perhaps the Romans had something. Boys are young animals. To attain the vigor and the endurance of the species they must during waking hours be in almost constant motion. Notice how very young boys wrestle and tumble over each other like puppy dogs, and how boys approaching the teens will race from one end of a field to the other, prelude to more formal contests later on. There is much of vital education to be gained from athletics, as good coaches are never tired of pointing out.

There is even more to be learned from the variety of informal games that suggest themselves in a wilderness location. What is learned unconciously, and with joy and gladness, will remain long after the other kind has been poured out on some test and evaporated. The most essential education fosters maturity and wholeness, the integration of personality.

"In wildness is strength," Thoreau wrote. Summer camps have one of the most vital adjuncts to education—their unspoiled woods and fields.

A camp's activities should be nearly all indigenous, springing from the location itself. This is particularly true of a camp's games. They will be homemade games, adapted to the terrain, evoking a deal of imagination in their general design and rules.

The Farm and Wilderness Camps play traditionally on the first Saturday afternoon of the new season a game called Transportez-le-Bois. Its purpose is threefold: to help unify the cabin groups, to get the camp grounds cleaned up after the winter storms, and to build the tremendous bonfire which is always the climax of the Independence Day celebration.

For a boy like Jack Fox, this activity broke the ice, starting the process of integration with his cabin mates. From old boys Jack had heard about Transportez-le-Bois.

"Huh, you won't catch me getting hooked on that one. Tricky way for the camp to get its work done for free."

"Well, so what!" Frankie Ray retorted indignantly. "It's all in a day's fun. One of the best games of the season."

"What, hauling all that old limb wood up to the Catamount Clearing, and dragging up the old shed roof that covered the cabin firewood? Not my idea of fun. You must got a wire loose somewhere."

The skit at the end of announcements won him over. As the host for the day finished speaking, there was a sudden clatter on the dining room porch. The door opened and two bewildered looking Frenchmen in berets and dark glasses stumbled in.

"Vair eez zee camp?" the first one asked the host. "Ve valk so many kilometres in zis forêt. Ve get—how you call it, mon vieux?"

But the second Frogeater had discovered an audience. "Aah. So many garçons. Zees *eez* zee camp, no?"

Then began a long parley addressed to the audience, a discourse in which the loquacious pair interrupted each other frequently, or one took over until his companion broke in again. From this discourse, replete with puns ranging from bad to worse, some in English, some in fractured French, it appeared that the two strangers were from the United Nations. They had been sent up for the weekend to "a camp vair eez lots of vood." Their assignment was to teach American boys an old Gallic game, "très exotique." It had some funny rules. To play it you needed wood, special kinds of wood. It had to be deadwood—limbs, old logs, boards, anything you could find in the whole area around the cabins. You brought it up to a set of locations along the road at the top of the Catamount Clearing. Each cabin had its own location, indicated by the name of a French mountain or a river or a region in France. "Eef you bring in brush, you pile eet viz zee—how you call eet?—zee butt ends to zee road."

Old-timers who had worked in other years on trucking these gigantic piles to the Fair Grounds to build the bonfire appreciated this reminder of careful stacking.

Jack was caught up in the audience participation. When the puns were bad the whole dining room groaned; when they were good they booed. Now and then a real "wing-dinger" brought the house down. The boys whooped and howled, slapping each other on the back. The pseudo-French names given the staff who were to share in the activity often pointed up some foible or a special interest of the counselor.

The introduction, like the similar skits before other games, was different each year. Sometimes the strangers would be Egyptians, or Swedes, or almost anything which offered good chances for puns. But in with the fun and the laughter, the game was described and its rules made clear.

The game itself was like the introduction. Though it served a practical purpose, the game was dressed up in such a fanfare of foolishness, with the two "Frenchmen" oh-ing and ah-ing at each big load that came up, or engaging other staff in scraps of conversation, that Jack forgot the heat of the day or the exertion of walking some oversized log out of the woods with a cabin mate beside him at one end and two more at the other end. His back and arms were smudged with dirt; sweat poured off the tip of his nose. The piles grew with every new load. The next cabin's pile had grown beyond expectation. The boys had discovered more brush at one end of the Timberlake Farm. Jack's cabin equalled this by hauling up those boards from the collapsed roof of their little woodshed.

The counselors in charge of the game knew just when to stop it. The decision brought forth a torrent of frenzied French from the two visitors, who, it seemed, were in favor of continuing until all the piles were the same height. The argument went on until all the boys had assembled to enjoy it.

"But, my friends," the host of the day explained, "you judge the piles on different things. This one, for instance, is the roundest. Here's one that is the most woody. Over here is another that's the most artistic. The next is the most dramatic. Over there—well, we look them over together, yes?"

So it went. This trio scrutinized each pile and found it to excel in some respect. By this time the old five-gallon milk cans of bug juice with their clinking ice had arrived from the kitchen. The boys formed lines to each, tossing their paper cups into trash boxes beyond, or returning to get refills. Some years there were cookies with the bug juice; some years there was neither. But still the game went on. It evoked strenuous effort; it gave one a feeling of belonging; it made one feel good to have had his part in clearing the camp area for the summer's other games and activities; and that bonfire on the Fourth would really roar!

Another early-season game is a treasure hunt. This may be dressed up a bit differently and run again late in the season when campers have acquired knowledge of natural science. One of the objectives of the early-season games is that of acquainting newcomers with the whole area of the camp, enabling old-timers, distributed through the "teams," to share their knowledge of the terrain. Clues this first time are generally easy, and such as new boys might know also. Later on, the clues will be more tricky, though the range of the hunt may be more restricted. Sometimes they require a council of all the pack while the more knowledgeable members settle some disputed point.

"Under the larch tree just before the hairpin turn above the Trading Post," the clue read. What was a larch tree?

"Oh, I got it," a slender, freckled-faced boy called out. "Larch is another name for a tamarack. It looks like a pine, but in the fall the needles turn yellow and fall off. It's not a real pine."

"Oh, yeah? Who says so? I never heard of it," someone objected.

"I'll prove it to you. It's in my Scout manual. Wait here and I'll get it."

The boy was off down the path. He returned shortly to point with a grimy finger to a small illustration labeled, "American tamarack or larch."

Another clue read, "Look in the clump of Christmas ferns at the base of the granite cliff the White Diamond trail passes as it leaves the plateau above camp."

Somebody had observed the granite cliff that the trail over the Ridge passed just as it started climbing. Somebody else knew what a Christmas fern was. In a few minutes, everybody knew.

Treasure hunts are more fun when there are not too many participants. For a camp of a hundred youngsters this delightful game would be impossible if the group were not broken down into eight or ten teams starting at different points, the older ones being given a rugged section the others skip. Laying this complicated trail is as much fun as running it later. Several Counselor Apprentices may be taken along for the experience of laying a trail. In the area over which the trail will range, what are the natural features to which attention should be drawn? When a clue has been hidden, how must it be described so as to be accurate, distinguishable from other similar hiding spots, yet not too wordy? If the whole group of Counselor Apprentices has been involved, the head of the camp may himself lay out a trail for these Counselor Apprentices the next week as a sort of celebration.

A gorge with a mountain torrent rushing down over moss-covered rocks is a favorite spot for such a purpose. At the end, an undiscovered pool where all may strip and splash, or slide down some slippery rock falls will be treasure enough, with a chance to sit in a spot of sunlight and discuss the theory and practice of laying treasure trails.

For a big group, a nature scavenger hunt is easier to set up. Each team can subdivide into smaller groups, fanning out to find as many as possible of the long and ingenious lists of natural objects. Where, for instance, can you find little black pollywogs, to be presented still healthy in a jar of water, then returned to their natural habitat? Every boy probably knows that these wigglers congregate in numbers along the sandy margin of the pond where the sun strikes it. And red efts can be found on damp woodland trails. Red efts are very particular. The crew that brings one in must also be armed with the strange story of the eft's transformation.

Maidenhair ferns likewise have their own special haunts. Only *one* frond can be presented by a team. These dainty woodland beauties are not so common that one can pick them wholesale. For this reason a plant like the walking fern, which most groups will know by this time, can be found in a rocky glen at the end of the lake. This species never appears on a scavenger list. And you must have done some climbing along the near side of the Ridge to know where you can find a "seed of a white oak." The hair from the mane of Winnie the Shetland pony requires that you understand how to approach her without starting her running.

A Mille Fleur feather is a commonplace to those who have been caring for members of the poultry clan. The little chestnut brown feather with its black edge and white tip could never be mistaken for a feather from any other bantam. So it goes with some forty items, all of which contribute choice bits of information to the eager players. The nature of the learning process being what it is, chances are that these vital tidbits and their correlative pieces of information will stay with the learners long after irrelevant facts acquired under duress have vanished without a trace.

Other homemade games like that called kingdoms, and a complicated game played some years and known as Chinese chess, offer various kinds of learning, besides the boon of running and crouching and crawling as the situation may demand.

The game called spy night, played late in the season when darkness steals on early, teaches the participants much about mastering complexities of organization. One is not so inclined to buckle, it may be, when he has had the experience of sorting out the various duties and functions of far patrols, in patrols, palace guards and spies who may do one thing but not another. Haven't they been briefed by their patrol captains, learning thus to take orders from somebody who may not happen to be a pal? Haven't these patrol captains, veterans of at least one previous spy night, warned them of the routes a spy may take to reach the "palace," or the ruses he may work on the unsuspecting? And haven't they learned that even the captain of a patrol, who has spent the early hours of evening briefing the group, may turn up missing when the game begins, thus conveying the dismaying fact that *he* is a spy! Thank heaven the assistant patrol leader proved loyal. What if he, too—a thing which has never happened—should prove to have been tapped out very secretly earlier as a spy? Everyone had better be prepared to operate on his own. What a test of judgment and self-reliance; and what a chance for natural leadership to emerge.

Another popular Saturday afternoon all-camp game is stagecoach.

Despite opinions held by some, an important part of one's early education involves putting forth at times the very last ounce of energy one has and *not giving up*. This old-time favorite, like spy night, offers many occasions when one must rely on his own wits and bulldog tenacity.

Watching the trend of the ingenious little farce used after announcements some Saturday noon to introduce the all-camp game, certain old-timers may suddenly cast a knowing glance at a crony across the table. This is it — stagecoach this afternoon. Terrific! Revised and refined each year since the original rules suggested by the counselor who introduced stagecoach, the rules of this exciting game are complicated. The Good Guys, in two separate groups, are stationed at opposite ends of the long strip of open woods through which the game is played. A third group, the Bad Guys, are in between. They are the raiders, the outlaws, who try to intercept the stagecoaches as they ply between the two groups of Good Guys. The stagecoaches are represented by groups of boys, or just one or two boys, trying to run number-ten cans of green apples through the brigand-infested territory. The cans contain what their label states, gold bullion at two hundred points; animal pelts at fifty points; wheat at thirty; smallpox at minus one hundred.

Played all of a long summer afternoon, it calls forth countless clever strategems, daring escapes, and dramatic encounters. It can also furnish lessons in stamina or shrewdness, or dogged determination.

The ruse of sending a relatively valueless consignment guarded by a band of "riders," while a lone boy carrying the gold bullion runs swiftly along the flank, is a common one. It is not always spotted in time. Such a ploy had drawn off the main body of the Bad Guys. One youngster in the raiders' party noticed from the corner of his eye a distant form dart swiftly from behind one tree trunk to another. Dashing down to see what this was, he found himself in full pursuit of a can of — whatever it was, it might carry the deciding points of the game.

Cut off from a direction parallel to the main group of raiders, the fugitive plunged on down to a swamp. Soon both boys were splashing from hummock to hummock. Nothing worrisome about this, since they were both in the usual camp uniform, a pair of shorts. Big hummocks like this, taken at top speed, and in imminent danger of a spill, can be exhausting.

Soon both boys were panting. To the pursuer it seemed as if his chest would split. His heart pounded. He could go no farther. Yet there was that elusive shipment of gold — probably it was gold, just ahead of him. If he stopped even for a moment to catch his breath the fugitive would put a second hummock between them and then escape. Keep at it, keep it up, keep — He could go no more. His legs were lead; they refused to move. He flopped down on a hummock in the sunlight, his arms flung wide, his mouth open, his chest heaving.

At this moment the boy ahead of him threw himself down, too. "Jeepers, it's good you fell out, I couldn't go another step and I was just going to give up."

Years ago at a party in Beirut a German ex-Army officer from the First World War was talking amiably with his opposite number from the British forces in the same campaign, Gallipoli. "You know," the German said in a confidential tone, "you British saved our lives, literally saved our lives. I mean it. Ach! We were out of ammunition; we had no further reserves; the Turks were demoralized; we had almost completed plans for giving up and stealing away. Then to our amazement that morning when you raised the siege we found the Allies had left. Why did you do it?"

Why? The British commanding officer as a boy hadn't played stage-coach.

6

The explorers' club

To a child the wilderness is enchanted indeed. With a little guidance his eyes will see the wonders in every copse, the mystery in every leaf and blade of grass. His ears will catch the small sounds in the woods. He will like the smooth "feel" of the yellow adder's tongue. The puckery taste of the choke-cherry will prove intriguing. The drop of sweetness in the lobe of a wild columbine blossom will please him mightily. And the fragrance of the summer fields after a rain will fill him with delight.

But there are pitfalls for the counselor presenting this kind of magic to the keen senses of the young. Too many have already become the victims of uninspired "education." Dull people have already taken his campers on "nature walks," or perpetrated "nature classes." Despite some very wonderful people in these fields in public education, the Farm and Wilderness Camps prefer to avoid the whole tattered terminology. We never go on "nature walks"; we take hikes to follow a deer run, or to see if the bottle gentian in that swampy meadow shows its vivid blue yet to match the sky.

Instead of "taking nature study," boys at Timberlake join an Explorers' Club at the start of camp. Its members build dams to pen up fingerlings and, hopefully, to watch them grow. The Explorers set up aquaria as near like the natural habitat of the expected guests as can be managed after close observation. Members of the Club spy shamelessly on the private lives of frogs and turtles. They trace the runnels in an ant "palace." They set up catchy signs along trails near camp, pointing out noteworthy items of local flora and fauna, this after checking their facts in the Club's array of manuals with their absorbing colored pictures.

The Club sponsors many afternoon excursions. Several different groups, depending on the number of knowledgeable leaders the Camp can muster, may set out on a fine afternoon. Anticipation is keen; the announcements at lunch have seen to that. The objectives are clear in everyone's mind. Perhaps the interest of one group has been caught by the chance of seeing some beaver at the headwaters of a little brook where earlier trips have reported activity by these engineers of nature. The hikers will be far from blind to all kinds of other interest along the way: the outcropping of schist that sparkles in the sun as the boys swarm over a wide ledge; the successive belts of spruce, then maple, yellow birch, and beech; the owl pellets under a giant hemlock; the changes in vegetation as the group comes down again into lowland; the rank growth of tall cone flower and the magenta joe pie weed where sun and swamp combine to provide the right conditions. The expedition will not be too seriously disappointed if they fail to see a single beaver. They will have studied the evidence of the beavers' work; they will have marveled at the instinct which underlies the engineering skill with which they build their dams and flotation canals.

Another group of explorers may meanwhile have climbed to the ledge high above the Plymouth Valley, a ledge known in camp as Mad Morgan's Potato Patch. The view of the lake, the whole valley, the camps and their myriad activities will make this breathtaking climb exciting, and who knows what wonders one may see along the way? One can always bring home some of the little red-tipped lichens from the ledges, or some shelf fungus on which to inscribe the names of the participants in the expedition. And one has had a preliminary experience in following the markings of a not-always-simple trail.

The most exciting trip of the afternoon is an exploration of Floating Island Cove. "Take along some number-ten cans for frogs and salamanders; and if you're wearing shoes, leave them at the cabin."

The advice in the announcement was hardly necessary: everyone knew the fun of splashing around in the warm, shallow water of the Cove;

stories of breaking through the edge of one of the islands of matted vegetation were passed on from one expedition to the next.

The whole Catamount Cabin opted to go on this expedition. Larry Somers, the new boy from Arizona, had never seen anything like a floating island. "Does it fly, too?" he asked incredulously.

This was a new experience to the eager twelve-year-old from the arid West. As the canoes threaded the narrow passage into the Cove, they passed into a different world. Larry pushed the dark hair away from his eyes and stared in unbelief. There before him, steaming in the sun, was a little bay rimmed by birch and hemlock. The greater part of the surface of the water thus enclosed was covered with a floating mass of vegetation, a flat land of wild cranberry and sphagnum moss fringed with alders, with a channel of blue water here and there where a part of the island had broken off. Around the whole mass a wide arc of open water showed, with the remains of an ancient beaver house at one side. This all had to be explained to Larry, along with the warning about "holes" in the island.

"Take off your shorts," someone suggested, as Larry's canoe sought a good landing spot. "You'll probably fall in." A glance at the other canoes showed the boy that all were prepared, hopefully, perhaps, for this eventuality.

The squash of the spongy growth of cranberry and sphagnum felt great under one's feet. The day was hot and sunny and still, at least in the Cove. The counselor cautioned the group to watch where they stepped, showing the uninitiated several pitcher plants with their curious leaf traps for unwary insects. A red-winged blackbird scolded them from a branch of alder leaning over the water.

"He's got a nest over there. Can anybody spot it?" the counselor asked. "Keep away from that next bush. There's a big yellow-jackets' nest in it. See?"

From a safe distance the boys admired the growing bulk of the gray paper nest, with its busy inmates entering and leaving through the hole at the pendulous tip. One boy had been watching the modest brown bird that followed the red-wing.

"That's his mate, isn't it?" he asked. "She doesn't look like him at all."

There were other wonders on the island—the sun dew, another carnivorous plant that uses a sticky pad to catch its prey. And the turtles— painted terrapin—along the edges went plop into the water as the boys approached. Frogs were fun to watch. They dove straight down, their hind legs almost straight out behind them.

Back in the boats, the boys turned the prows down a long channel on the far side of the island. Larry noticed how the green of low-sweeping hemlock boughs were mirrored in the still water. Before the ripples from the first canoe broke the surface, the illusion was complete. These soaring hemlocks ran far down into shadowy depths. The canoes were lazy birds floating across feathery branches. Occasional sunken logs were dimly visible on the bottom. Now and then a rotting stump far below reached up almost to the bottom of the canoe. As the canoe floated into deeper water, the boy from the arid West marveled at the dim reaches below him. Slender, feathery water weeds waved in the sluggish current; clouds of minnows wove in and out through the watery forest, their bodies glinting when they caught the sun.

The big red orb of the setting sun was already caught among the tall tips of fir and hemlock along the western shore when this expedition began to think of returning home. Cans and jars were brimming with treasures. Everybody had fallen in at least once. To keep the shouting and disturbance at a distance from this delicately balanced world, the counselor had suggested swinging around by the sandy strip of shore at the entrance for a swim. This, of course, occasioned further delay; at the camp dock the last swimmers were being driven reluctantly out of the water as the returning fleet rounded the tip of Otter Point.

After some of the complex interrelations observable in a place like Floating Island Cove, older campers, boys in their early teens, will delight to dig out something of the science of ecology. They will read enough to talk learnedly of the intricacies of conservation. The problems of environmental control begin to challenge their thinking. At this point they will listen eagerly some evening to a knowledgeable visitor from the Natural Resources Board of the state, plying him with thoughtful questions until the staff in charge of the meeting finally calls a halt.

But active boys of nine to eleven or twelve, prime ages for instilling concern for the quality of wilderness, couldn't care less for these abstractions. Explorers below their teens, and many teenagers, too, are captured by the creativity and action involved in setting up a clay-lined pool below some spring in camp. When the pool can be made to hold water—this is easy if it catches the runoff from a spring—it will be stocked with frogs and turtles and salamanders and every variety of pond life the boys can catch. If the pond is in the shade, transplanted jack-in-the-pulpit and turtlehead may grace its shores. For a pool in the sun, campers will find cowslips and sensitive fern and other plants that like to get their feet wet.

Among constructive projects, that of building a raccoon cage with heavy wire and a tree to climb may catch the interest of another group. Under their auspices the local game warden may be invited to speak to the camp of an evening, explaining why the state requires a permit to keep wild animals even for a few days. The visit of such an official is sure to generate wide and sustained interest. In fact, this patient functionary's endurance may give out long before campers' questions have all been answered. The curiosity of boys about animals seems to be inexhaustible.

Other approaches to a later, more formal study of nature may involve building a large terrarium, or a vivarium for insects. Various types of ecological fact must be considered in planning such an approximation of a natural habitat. Its construction will spark many an afternoon expedition. The vivarium, being smaller, so its inhabitants will not be completely lost to view, is often a project for just a couple of boys, or perhaps a loner. "Collecting" trips may involve just a boy or two without a staff member along, except that such a man's advice will probably be sought before the trip and carefully followed where it is found to apply.

One of the most effective approaches to nature study in the Camps is through a safari. The term is something of misnomer, since these camp expeditions of the latter part of the season are never destructive of natural habitat or its denizens; nor do they upset the balance of nature as the ones whence the name is taken may do. But the name has the advantage of romance: it suggests far-off places, a dash of danger; and adventure with strange new forms of wildlife.

There are various kinds of safaris now at camp, all stemming originally from those of the Explorers' Club.

One type is the work safari, in which the boys who have been most interested in work crews through the early part of the summer go to some shelter at a distance from Camp. Then they settle in for several days and do a job on the area. The shelter's roof may be patched if it needs it; bunks are trued up; perhaps a new fireplace built; a dam may be thrown across the stream that usually flows by such a shelter; or perhaps a splash pool reopened; a supply of wood is bucked up and stacked under the wide eaves. But all of these activities stop at the discovery of a thrush's nest in the neighboring thicket, or a wary trout in an upstream pool.

The campcraft safari seeks out new areas for hikes, with a view to exploring new natural wonders and checking the best spots for overnight shelters. The boys map the region using the appropriate geodetic quadrant; they blaze trails and mark them on the maps. If a leader knows how to use a transit, the group may take surveyor's instruments along to figure elevations.

An Indian safari uses in a practical way all of an older boy's accumulated knowledge of natural foods. It is something of a survival hike. Boys who have shown they can take it are sent out with a topflight campcraft man and some assistant leader. They carry little beyond moccasins, a knife and breech cloth, matches, fish hooks, a blanket and a few raisins, hunks of cheese, and some dried apricots. They "bushwack," or they make their way to some known camping spot and devote themselves to just staying alive. The challenge of this sort of experience for selected boys always brings them back with a bit of swagger and endless tales of adventure, plus a ravenous appetite that takes several days to satisfy! The most responsible campers may be allowed to take such a trip alone, that is, without a staff member.

The natural science safari is set up like an expedition of the Smithsonian Institute, only, of course, bigger and more carefully planned! Of the probably eight boys selected, one or maybe two are interested in mapping and geology; a couple in birds; two or three in mammals and reptiles. Someone may take on the survey of the area's ecology, trying to find out how the animals and plants serve each others' needs.

A whole afternoon may be spent in discussion and preparation for this hike, in getting science gear together, poring over route maps and agreeing on the type of tarps to take along for shelter. Everything is weighed and packed in the smallest possible compass, for packs are bound to be heavy at best on this sort of expedition.

The trail on one such expedition led through camp and up over the ridge, through a crossroads of Plymouth Village, past an old cemetery. Then it plunged into real wilderness. This was, however, a wilderness which had closed in on the earlier works of man; the network of trails followed former logging roads. The occasional cellar hole and the long stone walls running through what was now deep woods marked where old farmsteads had been. At one point the boys on the trip stopped to explore what had once been a thriving little crossroads village, now overgrown with vines and brush. Trees a foot through grew out of its cellar holes.

The party reached Pickerel Pond in the late afternoon, tired, hot, and dirty. Leaden packs were set down gratefully. Rid of shoes and shorts, the boys headed for the break in the fringe of alders along the shore which the old-timers knew indicated a beach of sorts.

The rest of the hours to bedtime were filled with housekeeping details, such as getting the meal, setting up the camp, unpacking equipment, and organizing the watches. There were four each night, beginning at ten, when all was quiet and the fire burned low. These were the highlights of the trip. Each night for two hours a boy sat alone, listening to the noises of the night, savoring the smells wafted on lazy air currents, and recording all this as best he could with pencil in the darkness on a big pad of paper.

Here was a new area to most of the group. It was curious to see the way the character of the plants and trees changed with differences of soil and moisture. Hardwoods gave way to pine and spruce on the upper slopes or where a gravelly knoll appeared. Occasional low places were the habitat of swamp maples, willow and alder. A fringe of closed gentian ran up the swales. Chipmunks scuttled away from tumbled rocks in dry places; while a black snake, several kinds of frogs, and a turtle or two were flushed out of the swampy rivulets that made their way down to the pond.

The campfire that second night was mostly devoted to learning what the various groups had discovered. The pair interested in mapping and geology had made the widest circuit, and gave a description of the surrounding terrain and the types of rock in the basin of which the pond was the bottom. The ornithologists had spotted several red-wing blackbirds, always beside a swamp or a sluggish stream. What attracted them to such places? What was their food? Evidence of mammals was everywhere. The group agreed on a stalking expedition that night to try to catch the beavers at work. The two boys "on mammals" were equipped with a flash camera and hoped to get pictures. Arrangements were made also for some stargazing afterwards from a raft and from a point of land where there seemed to be a clearing.

It was almost lucky it rained the next day, so full had the day before been and so late the hour of retiring. The counselor in charge suggested that everybody sleep late. A breakfast of sorts would be ready as safari members appeared. Mostly the boys enjoyed the luxury of stretching at length in snug pup tents, eating peanut butter sandwiches and dozing or staring out at the rain-swept pond. A few hardy souls emerged from the tents to take a quick swim, then splashed through the dripping woods, not minding at all the sudden showers they shook from every overhanging bough.

In the afternoon it cleared. Lunch over — good thick vegetable soup and plenty of it — the expedition got to work again, each group continuing and completing its own part of the survey.

Our friend Larry Somers, agog with eagerness to explore this lush, rain-blessed country, had a second chance at a "watch." He had discovered the night before that what with listening for sounds, sniffing the night breeze for strange smells, and straining to see the occasional beaver that swam past in the middle of the pond, there was no time to concentrate on the personal things he had wanted to figure out. He got used to the occasional plop of a beaver hitting the water with his tail. The call of the hoot owl which had alarmed him the first night at camp seemed here romantic and mournfully beautiful, the veritable voice of the wilderness. Other sounds he heard, as had the rest — a fox barking on the distant hillside, the grunt of a bear, the squeak of meadow mice near at hand, the sound of deer coming down to drink. Several times he heard the hard breathing of what must have been deer close at hand in the undergrowth behind the camp.

One of the contributions the Farm and Wilderness Camps try to make to their campers and to the country's need is that of a group of youngsters sensitive to nature's wonders, her beauty, her vital importance to the whole nation. A steady stream of ardent conservationists "graduate" from the Camps. As in so many other areas, population increases make the struggle against deterioration of environment a race against time. Camps in general have an unrivaled opportunity to play a key role in this realistic type of education. But it requires a carefully considered approach to nature to foster the deep and abiding interest on the part of every citizen which is needed to win this race.

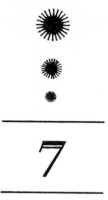

7

Security is feeling needed

One has only to imagine the life of the Bishops, the family who gave their name to the Bishop Mowing and the clear, cold Bishop Spring, to realize how deprived the modern urban generation is, and how necessary for wholesome growth is some farm and wilderness camp. With the Bishops, children were a tremendous economic asset, essential to the running of this small community. One didn't have to look around for meaningful work these children might do; there was work of all kinds clamoring to be done. It had to be handled or the family could not continue. Even the little bit the four-year-old could contribute was a help.

Consider how lucky he was, this four-year-old. Mother couldn't get to it to sweep the floor of the woodshed each day, and father was certainly too busy. But if that floor wasn't swept, men coming in from outside would track an increasing amount of dirt into the kitchen. Dirt? The four-year-old of himself couldn't care less about dirt. It was his natural element. But his parents and his older siblings seemed to think clean floors were important. They depended on him to do this job. He was part of the smooth running of the whole enterprise. They praised his good work. They needed him. He could see for himself that they wanted him. He was secure. Here life was stripped down to its simple elements, the necessities; no one was pretending to anything. Needs were self-evident. In this sort of environment you could believe the older people. There was no need for hypocrisy on their part, or for pretending to be what you were not.

Something of this simple, self-evident necessity of living resides in most of the work at Camp. Here is a reasonably self-sufficient community, clean, vigorous, direct, and honest. Needs are self-evident. They spring either from the necessity of eating — work in the gardens or on the farm — or they stem from the need of keeping warm and dry — the building of shelters or retarring of roofs, the cutting, splitting and bringing in of firewood.

The advantage of getting from here to there and back expeditiously makes self-evident the need for good paths and rustic bridges over runnels from woodland springs. Satisfying youth's curiosity about the ways of the furry and feathered crowd leads naturally to work on spacious pens and little fishponds. The satisfaction of man's esthetic craving sparks a season's work on a trout pool at a convenient spot on a tumbling brook. Perhaps, also, man's primitive love of water and mud and vigorous action in both these elements enters into the lure of building dams. This and the attraction of activity which stretches growing muscles in company with respected peers. In fact, the attractions of building a dam are so many and complex as to make this type of enterprise a natural for a group of boys. The First Lodgers will spend a morning after a night of heavy rain absorbed in damming the little stream that flows through their cabin area. Older boys will set in motion some enterprise of great pith and moment on the stream that comes down from the old Indian Village. In fact, a season spent in the varied activities involved in throwing a log or a cement dam across this stream may be the most rewarding and reasonable experience of a whole summer.

When to the natural attraction of slopping around in mud and water can be added the fascination of a cement mixer, even an old one, prone to clunk to an unexpected stop now and then, the combination is just about perfect. A group of fourteen-year-olds, some of whom can bring good muscles and the skills of work experience to the project, find an irresistible attraction in the problem of damming up the little stream that flows from the aforementioned old Indian Village into Plymouth Lake. This particular dam is near the mouth of the stream. The object is to create a sizable pool to add to the beauty of the long, low brown-stained building called Brooksend, center for many an evening of stories, or a far-ranging discussion, or some music followed by that perennial favorite, bug juice and cookies.

The site of the dam is a scene of perpetual activity. The crew of six knows just what each is to do. There is almost no lost motion. Of the pair who are nearest the mixer, one boy, evidently the "engineer," assumes a professional stance beside this ancient piece of machinery and peers into the greedy maw, watching the measured sand and bluish cement powder take form. He takes up a pail of water, pouring it carefully into the mixer, ready to stop when judgment says the mix is right. The water boy has on work gloves, but little else. He is covered with smears of drying cement. He looks remarkably like our old friend, Jack Fox. In fact, it *is* Jack. How come our protester of the first week has the key position on this work crew? The energy and quick physical competence which got him into endless trouble at home have here led to his recognition as an able and responsible operator. When because of approaching darkness, the emphasis is on getting the job done, Jack is the recognized expert. But it has taken some doing earlier in the season for him to achieve this sort of recognition.

A second and third boy with wheelbarrows wait at the ready for the load which will be packed into the waiting forms. Where the dam is already completed, a boy is prying off the forms. Two more workmen are busy nailing up the new forms for tomorrow's stint, lining up their work with stakes and string.

Ordinarily there would be a projects counselor busy with many things — tamping the mix into the forms; casting an eye into the mixer to judge the readiness of the mixture; or checking the arrival of sand, small stones and the precious bags of cement, trucked in by another crew. But these boys work together with no problems requiring counseling, or outside construction skills. Considering the time of day, one can understand the counselor's absence. He has some other duty, for it is evening.

The deepening dusk of an August night finally forces the crew to wash out the mixer, cover it over, slosh some water over the wheelbarrows, and themselves, then head down toward Timberlake, talking earnestly about the day's accomplishment.

Started in the morning after Meeting for Worship, the job became so exciting that the crew elected to return after rest hour, then came back to finish pouring after supper. These seniors at Timberlake, on the threshold of manhood, are for the most part secure enough in their roles. Self-confidence, not to mention a bit of swagger, sticks out all over them. Security is not always the major benefit campers derive from physical work. They are approaching the time when satisfaction in a job well done can loom large in their lives. The creative urge features also in the interest boys take in such an environment-changing project as a new dam, a bridge, a flight of steps, a log shelter. Growing muscles respond willingly, even joyously, to this chance to test them. And, as always, the fun of doing something together lures the laggards.

Not the least involved is our friend Jack Fox. His cynicism has given way to eager interest. His alienation has changed to involvement. His scoffing at everything has yielded to deep respect for certain counselors at Timberlake. Through catching their attitudes, this respect has begun to deepen into a sense of reverence for life, for qualities of fineness he has discovered in peers and elders. He has come to regard nature with reverence, as something precious which must not be destroyed, rooted up, littered, or wantonly cut down.

Jack is not reflective; he is an activist. His sturdy frame craves challenge, excitement, the spice of danger. Boredom and the softness of suburban life could dispose him to violence later on if no socially acceptable outlet came to hand. At camp Jack is finding challenge. He enters into a project like the dam with his whole personality. In some of the more exacting hikes he finds the excitement he needs, and the spice of danger. The boy is far from sprouting wings, or even from being yet securely on the road to an integrated personality, but he's gaining!

Like many another city youngster, Jack may be regarded as underprivileged, or disadvantaged. Compared to the wholeness of life their farm offered the Bishop children, young Fox has been cheated. He has had no opportunity to feel a useful part of the small society which is the family. Nearly everything in the way of useful chores has been taken over by automation. The sense of security proffered to even the youngest of the Bishops could not be his. Being by nature forceful and eager to make his impression on his surroundings, the deprivation of his suburban culture turned him in upon himself. The other-centeredness open to the Bishops resulted from their sense of contribution to the welfare of the rest of the family. It led to a definite other-centeredness which is one of the marks of maturity. For Jack and thousands like him, there was no ready way to grow out of the natural self-centeredness of childhood. The result we see around us in society today, in the divorce rate, in the police courts, in the senseless struggle and violence where there should be peace and cooperation.

For a new boy it takes a while to see the reason for the morning cleanup at each cabin and around the whole camp. These humdrum tasks offer little of creativity, nothing of excitement; only the companionship of others condemned to the same servitude, which somehow escapes ever being regarded as servitude.

One newcomer in a cabin is generally absorbed rather easily into the system. But two or three new campers can cause difficulty. Then a cabin council may be called by the counselor, or, better, asked for by a couple of the old boys who know something is wrong. The whole matter of chores may be called into question. Why not live in a mess? What's wrong with a mess?

Some old-timer will remember an occasion when he needed a jack-knife quickly for some job he was doing; or an AP (all-purpose) neckerchief for a trip he had suddenly found he was on. His trunk was a mess, and he delayed half a dozen others while he searched.

"But if we're gonna do chores, and if we're gonna clean up so we'll know where a thing is when we want it, then why not get on the stick and get some organization into it? If everybody gets into it, the whole job needn't take more than a few minutes. Then it's done for the day." This counsel from an old-timer began to make sense.

"One year we had skin infections here because nobody cared about cleaning out the cabins and there was no inspection system. I had to stay home from a hike, and I couldn't even go in swimming." The Voice of Experience again.

The newcomers may not have been immediately convinced, but these bits of evidence were hard to refute. So they went along with the system, reluctantly at first, then gradually with some degree of pride in the smoothness and efficiency of a shared operation.

The morning cleanup chores that go on every day in each cabin before breakfast, and which must be done with dispatch and smooth efficiency or the cabin is late for the meal — these have an importance beyond just getting a necessary job done. Everyone must make his bed, and straighten up his gear. Somebody must sweep; someone must pick up around the outside of the cabin, perhaps check the paths nearest this little family center and take any rubbish up to the big box by the camp road. Unconsciously, Jack Fox began to lose his opposition to this daily ritual. Some of the benefits beyond the job itself began to make themselves felt.

For the past few years Timberlake has set up a comparable set of chores to involve the whole camp in crews of four for twenty minutes right after breakfast each day. The whole place becomes a beehive of activity. One crew starts sweeping the dining room, scarcely waiting for the last diners to wash down their bacon and eggs. Another crew starts bringing in wood for the woodboxes: chunk wood from the neatly stacked pile outside; kindling from squaw wood gathered in the surrounding forest and sawed or broken up. If the staff has been foresighted enough to park cars in the area by the Trading Post, another crew will be washing and cleaning these machines, checking gas and oil. The Upper Lodge washroom gets a going over from still another crew, while a third foursome puts the staff rooms in order. Three kybo (privy) crews will see to toilet paper, lime, and sweeping out the various three-holers. A library crew, one member of which should be on the library committee, takes the old papers off the racks, sweeps and tidies up the place. A couple of paths crews will see to getting more sawdust on any section where the spongy cover, so pleasing to bare feet, may have worn thin. Everybody has a job, everybody except a pool of unassigned campers who may go their several ways if not called on in the first ten minutes. After campers become familiar with the routine of any job, they function almost as well if the staff member assigned cannot be present. It is cheering to see how efficiently a group will carry on by themselves. In this event, natural leadership comes to the fore.

But the core of the work program, the dramatic aspect of it, if that word can be used in this connection, lies in the morning jobs set up by the projects department. These projects are as diverse as a varied terrain and a far-flung plant can provide. Some of the projects have been discussed with staff and campers at the end of the previous summer. Trial balloons may have been sent up during the winter through articles in *The Interim*, the Camps' monthly news magazine. Correspondence has gone on also with staff; suggestions have been solicited from campers. Frequently a cabin group, or several buddies who were together the previous year and now share a common interest and a liking for one another's company, may offer a project. This is discussed with staff or the head of projects, any "bugs" in it eliminated, and the friends sign up to-gether.

These major projects appeal to the creative impulse in most of us. Building a dam, as remarked before, satisfies several urges. The little stream that runs down from the spring above the lower lodge offers end-less opportunities for small log and earth dams. Since this rivulet flows through the First Lodge area, it becomes the special province of the nine- and ten-year-olds.

Landscaping some interesting area, such as the open space around a building, provides new knowledge and skills. It may mean jeep trips to a distant part of the property to find just the right mossy stones, or to bring in some bunch berries or ferns not found in a given area. It takes an eye for symmetry and balance, a bit of judgment regarding color, as well as a knowledge of what will do well in shade, or what likes to have its feet wet. And those who like to give muscles a workout can do so with the transporting involved.

A section of rail fence is another possibility. This requires coopera-tion with a forestry crew to get out the logs and poles. Or perhaps the fencing crew elects to spend all its projects time on this one enterprise and have the experience of cutting and barking the poles itself.

Another major project, one which may require more than one sum-mer to complete, is that of putting up a log shelter. A bridge over a small ravine or across Paradise Pool to Paradise Island is a piece of construction with real challenge. (This Paradise Island bridge seems to last about five years. All we need is five such islands to provide a fine piece of rustic engineering every summer!)

Pasture clearance used to be an annual project. Each successive crew simply divided a section of old pasture into strips and proceeded to clear it. Then we got careless about keeping the tools properly sharpened, and before the staff realized the difficulty, interest in this useful enter-prise had been killed. But camp generations change fast. After a lapse of several years, we can begin again, *with sharp tools*. Particularly will this be purposeful now that the Camps are starting to build up the stock farm.

Every year the so-called TL Farm develops new and exciting proj-ects: a fence to be extended; a flight cage to be enlarged; another pond dug out on the spring overflow for some more ducklings; perhaps a new coop put up for the increasing bantam family. Sometimes a project like the Brooksend dam takes over and preempts the time planned for other activities.

This happened a few years ago when a group of boys suggested a flight of steps to replace the steep grade from the Main Lodge down the edge of the lawn to the hairpin turn. Slippery when wet, this stretch of lawn was good for a few laughs when campers found themselves sliding down the grade on the seat of their pants. But it was inconvenient, especially if you didn't want to miss the start of an evening game. The steps required laying tiles in a ditch along the edge of the lawn, cutting hemlock logs to length for risers, barking them, and digging out the shallow beds to secure their ends. Beyond where the ditch turned off into the woods the boys encountered rough going through a copse which hid a good-sized rock. The boys were incensed at the director's suggestion that they make a zigzag around this rock.

"What, and spoil that fine curve?" one boy asked indignantly.

"And that zigzag would always be there to let people know we copped out," another boy objected.

"Why don't we *dig it out* this afternoon?" a third workman proposed. "We could dig down on this lower side, scoop out a hole, then all of us together could pry the rock over into the hole."

"Sure," another boy offered, his eyes alight. "I'll work."

"So will I," another volunteered.

"Why don't we all come down here? OK, Brownie?"

All eyes turned to the counselor who was heading up the project.

"Sorry. I hafta be down for some lacrosse. I'm the only staff who knows the game this year, so —"

"Aw, we can get along without cha," the first boy remarked.

"Pro'bly make out better," another added in the bantering tone that showed affection. "He's always gettin' in the way. He might even get hurt."

They worked all afternoon, even ignoring the bell for afternoon swim. It seemed an almost impossible task on which the director himself looked in now and then. Shovels and picks and crowbars got a good workout. A shout went up when the big stone finally tottered over the edge of the hole dug to receive it and the route was clear for the wide-sweeping curve to descend without interruption.

The director was telling a colleague from an old-line sports camp about this episode.

"You mean they worked all day? And they pay to come to camp?" the older man asked incredulously. "How can you get them to work like that?"

Another director chuckled at the thought of his own campers. "How can you get them to stop?" he countered.

The work hike is one of the most popular. The best workers and hikers are chosen for such a trip, and they know it. The group that have set out in the old Packard from the Trading Post will by midmorning be hard at work on their dam. The great hemlock logs which make the bottom and top have been hauled down the slope with great effort and set in place. When the uprights are in and the chinking done, the dam will be ready for filling. But the work takes longer than anyone had estimated; on the last day they are still far from finished. It is voted to work that afternoon. After supper some of them are dead tired, and "sack out" for a couple of hours. The rest in relays, and with the light of several Coleman lanterns, keep at it until nearly midnight, the post-prandial nappers rousing up to join the work. But at last, at long last, it is done. They stand a few moments to contemplate their handiwork with bleary eyes, then shuffle off to sleep the sleep of the satisfied — and the utterly exhausted. This great effort is just once on a hike, but it makes possible a glowing — and liberally embellished — account the next day at lunch when for a waiting world they recount their exploits and generously invite later groups to have a swim in the gigantic pool they expect will form behind their dam.

Able leadership is important in every aspect of a camp. Particularly is it essential in work projects. Skilled, mature, sensitive leadership is not easy to find. Motivation in a work job is everything, for the activity, while richly rewarding, is by no means natural to all boys. One father, years ago, took me aside after he had seen some of the movies of work projects and confessed, "I don't see Garry in that bunch you had out there on the road gang. The boy's allergic to work."

A leader has to love his group of youngsters in order to establish the close rapport necessary to knit the four or five or six individuals into an effective unit. He must be able to kid the loud-mouth who prefers using his voice to using his muscles. He must be able to offer a word of encouragement to the diffident youngster who lacks coordination. The boy who is clumsy with tools must be helped, perhaps shown a particular operation several times before he masters it. But above all, the leader must be able to motivate the crew, must keep before them the way things will look when the job is done, and how others will admire it. It's the old story of the workmen digging holes in a stubborn soil. Some were just digging holes; others were preparing the spot for a great cathedral.

The projects counselor must also be able to sense when the time of natural fatigue signals the approaching end of an attention span. This time comes sooner with nine-year-olds, of course, than with those of fourteen. But even with quite young boys, if the project offers within itself variety and a chance to change jobs, and if the whole crew are convinced of its desirability, they can occasionally spend a whole morning and find it a thrilling experience. But such projects are hard to find for First Lodgers because a nine- or ten-year-old's lack of coordination makes it unwise to trust him with sharp tools. Jobs such as cleaning up an area, raking, carrying, transporting are ideal. Taking hay to the lake shelters by boat; resanding the Indian lore beach, carrying bushel baskets of sawdust to surface a council ring, getting the stones out of a special swimming area and building a wall with them to rim the shore — such are jobs a large group can do with a mature man in charge and several younger staff members to help.

Sometimes ingenuity can dress the project up with the aspects of a game. The best example at Timberlake, and this has spread now to the other Farm and Wilderness camps, is "Transportez-le-bois," noted in an earlier chapter.

For two successive years projects were rated the most popular camp activity at Timberlake. This surprising preference for projects over sports tells something about the staff who man these projects — and the counselor who has the responsibility for directing all this energy. It has much to say also about the satisfaction through work of the creative urge which has so little outlet for many city children. Though the youthful crews don't realize this, it says much for the opportunity it gives youth to reverse the usual relation of being always on the receiving end as a child, with little chance to make an adequate return. And it certainly addresses the general theme of security as a result of feeling needed.

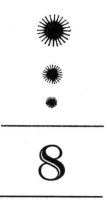

8

What a piece of work is man

*"What a piece of work is a man! how noble in reason! how infinite
in faculty! in form and moving how express and admirable! in action
how like an angel! in apprehension how like a god! the beauty of the
world! the paragon of animals . . ."*

Uttered by one of the most thoughtful of young men, and set to
music in one of the most youthful of modern musicals, this exalted view
of man's potential has some chance of fulfillment now that the new generation is rebelling against the hypocrisies and false values of their inheritance. A youngster who has come to realize that he *is* "in form and
moving express and admirable . . . the beauty of the world; the paragon
of animals," is more likely to achieve respect, even reverence for the complexity and the wonder of his body than is the boy or girl who accepts
uncritically the judgment of our Judeo-Christian tradition — strengthened
by the Puritan ethic and Victorian inhibitions — that the unclad body is
somehow a thing to be ashamed of. From this attitude of denigration of
the human body may stem some of the callous disrespect for it which
permits youth to abuse with drugs, alcohol and tobacco this most perfect and most beautiful of all creations. Therefore, one of the best de-
fenses youth can be given against the destructive, self-indulgence of our

hedonistic culture is this same respect for the body, its potential as a result of spartan living and simplicity of life.

If "sex without guilt" is one of the boons resulting from the modern iconoclasm, certainly freedom from clothes in physical activity away from the public eye should be another of its blessings. More general, it is to be hoped, will become the scene one encounters not only at Flying Cloud, where boys "live like Indians" but at the Timberlake water front and adjacent playing fields. Perhaps it is a cloudy morning, with a not-unpleasant nip in the air, a good morning for vigorous activity but not for long periods in the water. So activity at the water front takes the form of canoe practice, with "rowing for form" also offered the younger members of the lodge which is scheduled this morning for "Water Front and Physical Fitness." A few members of the group take advantage of a chance for criticism of a new stroke. They splash vigorously across the expanse of troubled water between the two docks, with a counselor shouting comments and encouragement.

On the two rafts is grouped the main part of the lodge, being briefed on a game about to take place in the water with the two rafts as goals. A whistle blows and the water is suddenly churned white with swimmers. A ball appears and disappears, then appears again far over toward one of the rafts. A shout and the pack is off after this tricky underwater swimmer. So the game surges from one dock to the other. Twenty minutes of play and another whistle blows. The boys draw themselves up on the two rafts, shouting wisecracks back and forth as commentary on the game.

When they have caught their breath, someone suggests a game of frisbee. First one form plops into the water, then several more, till the whole group is on its way to the shore. As the dripping swimmers emerge from the water they head for the wide playing field adjacent to the outdoor gym. Several frisbees are in motion at once, giving everyone just the blend of rest and action needed to counter the cool of the day. Soon a counselor calls from the outdoor gym, "First ten for the rope climb." Not ten but fully half the players break away from the game, but that's all right. Between the water-front staff and the physical fitness staff there is enough man power to get all the apparatus into action. A line forms by each item of the battery of homemade equipment. There is the rope climb, the chinning bars, the jumping pit, the overhead ladders, the parallel bars, the weight lifting equipment, and several elements of a rope course for the more enterprising. A tether ball at the end of the course takes up the slack. Soon this fascinating attraction is beset by too many customers. A counselor standing by heads the earlier arrivals back down to the water front.

There they may be given some land drill on form; then as the main part of the lodge reappears, the whole posse may set off across the cove, with a lifeguard in a boat on either side of the group of swimmers. Reaching the other shore, brown forms race along the path to the tip of this little promontory. The first in line has been instructed to head down to the water on a path opposite Paradise Island. Here two lifeguards are already in position. The first dozen racers dive into the water, swim down perhaps to inspect the steeply sloping bottom, then head back with the first boat to the distant docks. The second boat collects its complement of clustered heads; and as it leaves, a third boat swings into place, until all the boys who wish to take the distance swim are accommodated, and those who prefer a run will after a plunge or two head back around the cove by the path that follows the shore.

Meanwhile, another lodge, in from a morning of projcets, has preempted the water front and its staff; and perhaps the third lodge has shown up for a game of three deep at the playing field beside the Outdoor Gym. If there is still enough staff to man the stations of the Outdoor Gym, there will undoubtedly be customers there. There is endless variety, such variety as imagination and year after year of additions to homemade equipment can devise. Wrestling may go forward in an area of deep sawdust beside the Outdoor Gym. If it is a hot morning, the First Lodge may relax at an area of deep sand below a dam which in ordinary weather holds in check a pool whence water for sand modeling may be released.

Thus a whole morning may be spent in vigorous and in relaxed activity with enjoyment of the Fifth Freedom, freedom from clothes. A final quick dip at the three bell will be followed by a trip to the cabin for shorts and the trek up to the dining hall.

Meanwhile, another group will have been in the gardens. This, like the water front, is an isolated spot where one can savor the good earth with bare feet and get the warm sun over his whole body. This is a perfect way to add to one's "TL tan."

The girls at Indian Brook, and especially some of their counselors, covet this same freedom, so easy at Timberlake because of its greater isolation. Various expedients are tried to make this possible while shaking off the voyeurs which seem to be an increasing nuisance whenever the girls try to dispense with bathing suits.

At Tamarack Farm this clear-eyed generation, many of whom have the tradition of Timberlake or Indian Brook behind them, has resolved the matter of suits in a mixed group in a way which may seem daring to our clothes-bound culture, but which proves to be perfectly natural and obvious to the youngsters themselves. One year the first week each group enjoyed the customary suitless swimming at its own dock for an early morning dip and for a quick swim after work projects, just before lunch. But when the girls came over for a leisurely afternoon swim at the boys' dock, where most of the equipment is centered, both groups at first wore suits. Then the boys who had been brought up at Timberlake began to wonder why their lost freedom had to be lost. A serious discussion of the issue at Tamarack Farm's "Town Meeting" led to an agreement to wear suits for the first week, since some of the girls were uneasy about the Fifth Freedom in a mixed group. At the end of the first week any girls who were still uneasy about shedding suits should say so to the distaff side of the young couple who ran the water front. The identity of the protesters would not be revealed. If there was expression of uneasiness which the water-front director could not resolve by a little discussion, then the mixed swims would be suited, as in the past. To the relief of all, there was no protest. The group has swum for the most part unsuited ever since, at least after the first week. Sometimes a few of the girls will wear suits, but these generally disappear before the end of the season. Everyone does what he is easy with and there are no critical comments.

This evolution in attitudes is very like what happened at Timberlake in its first years. The boys were required to wear suits on weekends when parents might be present at the water front. Then several mothers discovered that their sons would not go into the water. They had either lost their swim suits or were so wedded to this new and delightful freedom that they preferred to wait until parents had left before going in.

"But why should they?" several mothers asked the director. "We don't care; we've seen boys undressed before this."

"But their sisters? How do you feel about them?"

"For my part," one mother replied, "if I have brought up my daughter in such a way that the sight of the male form without clothes is going to harm her, I'll figure that *I've* failed."

The others seemed to agree.

When the matter was brought up at powwow the next weekend, the boys' attitude was, "Well, we don't care if they don't care. So why bother with suits?"

Ever since, the Timberlake water front has been free of suits at all times, except for the occasional counselor who has no Farm and Wilderness tradition, and for whom this attitude is too new to take.

Tamarack Farm has a sauna, constructed over two summers by devoted crews who cut the logs for the building, squared them with loving care — successfully keeping feet and legs out of the way of swinging adzes — and built a Finnish bath that even the few Finn residents in the region approve.

For years the girls and the boys were carefully scheduled separately. Then one afternoon several years ago the girls got the fire started later than they expected, and were still inside when the boys arrived. The boys had a swim from the sauna dock while they waited, finally broke in on the girls. No screams of pretended fright; no off-color remarks, No earthquake! Since that time the Tamarack Farm sauna baths have generally been coed. This radical innovation has not proved sexually stimulating, nor has it had, as far as staff can judge, harmful effects in any way. It *has* cut down, so the staff in the boys' cabins says, on foul language and on snide remarks with double meaning. If the Finns can do it, why can't we, or isn't our culture that healthy?

This complete freedom in respect to clothes at the Farm has caused occasional repercussions beyond the Camp. When a thunderstorm overtakes a group at dinner, the lure of a warm shower in the downpour when the meal ends is too much for a few of the boys, maybe one or two of the girls. They strip off then and there and splash through the pools on the adjacent soccer field, playing tag and sliding through the puddles with shouts of glee.

It would have to be at that juncture that a delivery truck comes in, bringing with it the *mores* and attitudes of the outside world. The shock of this encounter, on the part of the driver, is retailed outside the camp, thereby adding to the regional mythology of these as "nudist" camps. Fortunately, over the decades the local people have come to respect the Camps, and realize they stand for much more than a 21st-century attitude toward clothes.

We understand that tourists driving by on the other side of the lake, half a mile away from the Farm dock, have complained to the state police about the suitless swimming. The response of these busy officers of the law has been, we are told, "Lady, it's their own water front, and too far away to see anything without field glasses, and nobody's obliged to use field glasses."

The Finns and the Indians are not the only races whose attitude toward the body differs markedly from our own. When we become conscious of comparative cultures, the origin of taboos, the irrationality of many cultural attitudes, we realize that our own unwholesome fixation on the body as somehow indecent is a sickness fortunately not widely shared among other cultures, though the dominance of our Western culture may make it appear so.

But we are recovering — fast, with the not-always-well-considered help of the new generation. One has only to look at some of the horrible pictures of "bathing costumes" fifty years ago to see how far we have come. In another few decades we may hope that children, looking at pictures of present-day beaches, may say, "But Daddy, why did people put clothes on to take a bath?"

Farm and Wilderness parents must either approve these attitudes or want badly enough some of the other things the Camps stand for to tolerate them. The Camps seem to attract a disproportionate number of parents who are doctors. These people have often approved enthusiastically of the Fifth Freedom as a means of strengthening health and the general physical stamina which is the best resistance to colds. They have commented on its contribution to mental health. More than once someone has speculated that the general honesty, frankness, and lack of pretense and concealment evident at the Camps — that all this unusual pattern may be connected with our habits in regard to clothes.

A study of comparative cultures leads to the suspicion that it could be — it just *could be* — that our culture is wrong in this regard; that the evil it has falsely imputed to nudism is in fact an evil in our own minds. It has cut us off from a health-giving, wholesome, and joyous practice in which children thrive and adults may find an honesty and straightforwardness, and even a spiritual surety and strength, that we grievously lack at present.

This "piece of work" that is man, how are we to become convinced of its wonder if by the fetish of hiding the body we deny and destroy some of its health and most of its godlike beauty?

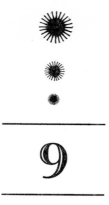

9

Claim everything

One of the greatest rewards in a camp director's life is that of hearing from boys of earlier generations. To discover that one has influenced some youngster in a way that has changed his whole pattern of life is reward enough for the countless times a director has tried his best to make clear some ideal, some principle, some point for reflection. At the time it may seem that no one heard. But then the director learns by chance and perhaps second or third hand, of some boy whose life has taken a different course because of an idea or ideal he found at camp.

And then another time came the knock at the door. "You probably don't remember me, especially with this shrubbery" — referring to a neatly-trimmed beard — "but I'm George Jessup, that mousy kid from 'way back in the early fifties. And this is my wife Anita." A charming young girl with a sensitive face and a gracious smile stepped forward to stand beside her self-assured husband.

"I guess you thought I was pretty much a total loss," George remarked during the subsequent conversation. "But you never can tell what a kid will pick up. From the times you spoke in meeting, or the times you talked to me alone, I remembered the parts I needed."

"He got a good deal," Anita observed. "I keep getting bits of it. So

I'm glad to meet you. Just the conviction that we are children of God, with some of the same creativity and hidden powers — this was worth the years at camp."

"Yes," George mused. "You probably don't remember the time you led a group of us on a hike up through Tinker Gorge. It was a TL tan trip, a surprise reward for having the best all-over tans."

"Oh, yes, that trip," Anita interrupted. "Our children are still hearing about it."

"The trip was the turning point in my life," George said. "You probably don't recall, but we came to a narrow part of the Gorge where the path crossed on a log to a ledge along the opposite side. You said that any who felt sure of themselves could walk the log; for the rest, there was a steep path down to the water's edge, and a crossing on mossy stones. 'But watch it,' you said. 'Those stones can be mighty slippery.' I stood a moment looking at the log. Then I sat down to take off my shoes. Most of us had left any such foolishness in the Packard, for after all, this was a TL tan trip."

"You know, George," the director broke in, "I do remember that very act of yours. I thought to myself, My Lord, the boy's just going to sit down and not take either way. Then you got your shoes off, and without a moment's hesitation you set out across that log. My heart was in my mouth, but you made it as nimbly as the two or three well-coordinated kids who had crossed before you."

"Yes," George replied, chuckling, "and you took the path across the stepping stones."

"Well, yes: I had more than myself to think of, and there's a difference between 1942 or thereabouts, and 1902 when I was born."

"I know. I was just kidding."

"You know what George was thinking while you were worrying about his just sitting there?" Anita asked. "George was saying over to himself, 'I am a son of God, and I can do anything I choose to do.'"

George pulled at his beard and grinned. "I guess that's true too. But I also thought of something you had quoted in Meeting some days before. I've looked it up since. It's from Malachi, Chapter 3, and it referred to tithing, but for me it applied to crossing that log. 'Try me, saith the Lord, and see if I will not open the windows of heaven and pour you out a blessing your measures cannot contain.' Maybe that's not exact, but it was like that."

"And it carried you across!"

"Yes, and back, too, later on. But what you said when I got across that first time has stayed with me ever since."

"What was that?"

"The kids cheered, but when you could speak to me without the others hearing — it was as we sat at the top of that little rock slide down into the pool — you said, 'You know, you could almost walk on water if you believed you could.'"

"Did I? Must be I had sensed something of what had gone on inside you."

"I was sure you had. You spoke more than once of the magic of believing. Anyway, that was the first turning point. I was still in the First Lodge. Then at the end of the two years in the Big Lodge, when I was eleven and twelve, another important event occurred. Remember that loud-mouth in the Otter cabin that year? I can't even recall his name now — mental block, I guess. But he had come back to camp after a couple of years away. I'd almost forgotten my old nickname of Droopy Drawers. He revived it, and it brought back painful memories. I asked him to lay off, but he'd found something he could bug me with; of course he kept it up."

"So that's what brought on the famous fight!"

"Yes. I never heard you as a Quaker condone fighting, but I was struggling to keep my belief in myself. If I hadn't turned that guy off, he could have destroyed me, and I knew it."

"I had figured from the other kids' account that there was more than met the eye. But you almost scared us to death."

Anita chuckled. "Me too, once when it happened the first year of our marriage. It hasn't happened since."

"No, and it won't. I've learned how to live with it. But then I didn't know what it was, except that when I got into a physical struggle of some sort, something snapped and I had to sit down quick. But with this bully, all I remember is that I'd said something real friendly like if he used that name again I'd paste over his big mouth with his teeth. Then I waded into him, making up in fury what I lacked in technique. But I was really no match for him. Then all of a sudden everything went blank. It wasn't from any blow. That heart specialist in Hanover finally worked it out. I guess he gave you the gory details. But Dr. Chambers, the man who first tended to me, was the most helpful. He explained it to me in simple terms, a rare type of faulty valve. He told me of other people who had serious handicaps. He said this didn't need to give me any trouble if I'd just control my emotions and keep out of situations where I had to put out a great amount of energy all at once."

"But I think it's the emotion that triggers it," Anita commented. "And that's the hardest part. Most of us don't control our emotions, we just control the outward show of emotion."

"Well, enough of me and my peculiarities. I'll just give you one more example of the dynamite in the philosophy you gave us. You used to say that what we pictured in our minds over a period of time as something we wanted very much, if we believed we could achieve it and worked on it in every way we could, sooner or later we would have it."

"The magic of believing, Claude Bristol," the director observed. "Well, it's true."

"I know it is. I've proved it over and over. Yet most people never discover this, and they go on living lives of quiet frustration."

"You know, I think you must be my most apt pupil." The director grinned. "It's great to hear this. Now, tell us, what's your 'one more example'?"

"Oh, that happened the next year, my first year in Senior Lodge. I'd been watching a cute little number from IB who came over to the Senior Lodge square dances. She was about the cutest I'd seen."

"That was before George had met me, of course." The self-assured smile Anita turned on the director was almost laughable, two of a kind.

"I don't remember seeing you in any of those squares. But then, I mostly remember kids who stood out in the dances for special grace or verve, or for clumsiness. That last wouldn't have been you."

"No, if I couldn't do a thing well, I couldn't bring myself to break into it. Afraid of making a fool of myself."

"But George is a good dancer," Anita said. "He's taught me most of those figures. And we found a folk-dance group soon after we were married."

"Well, I hung out on the sidelines for a long time," George went on thoughtfully. "I watched the dancers. I knew most of the figures, but somehow, there was enough of the old mousy First Lodger still in me to keep me out of things unless something made me put out extra effort."

"Like meeting this 'cute number' George speaks of. She must-a been keen, George." Anita flashed her husband a quick smile.

"Compared to Anita, of course, she couldn't rate. But I spent whole evenings following her around from a seat on the sidelines, or standing in the doorway. The staff tried to get me going, but no soap. Then I decided to use the same method I'd found worked on other things. I started picturing myself going up to the girl and asking her for the first dance. I'd watch for her to come in and get there first. Then I saw myself threading through the sets with her. No, I'm serious about this. It's just the way I worked it out."

"I know you're serious, George," the director explained. "I was smiling because somehow I'd never thought of applying these principles to a thing like a square dance. But why not?"

"Well, it worked, anyway. The next week I was right by the door when Janie came in. I did just as I'd seen myself doing. I marched up to her before any other guy got there and asked her how about the first dance. She seemed surprised. She hesitated a moment, then she looked at me and smiled. 'Jim Hermann was to meet me here, but he didn't show, so, the first dance? O.K.' It was as easy as that."

"Poor Jim hadn't worked on it in just the same way." The director chuckled.

"Oh, Jim came along later and Janie went off with him after a couple of sets. But that first dance, it was something I'll always remember. I forgot all about my big feet. I knew the figure, I had seen myself going through it perfectly, and I did. Kind of like walking on air."

"Floating on Cloud Nine, I'd call it," Anita commented. "I'm jealous."

"The thing I'm trying to bring out is that that freed me. It freed me from all sorts of fears or hesitations, self-doubt, the clumsiness a kid who's not sure of himself feels. From then on I gave Jim Hermann a run for his money. But the next year it was another cutie. By that time I was fooling around with what has since become my lifework."

"What are you doing, George? We haven't got onto that."

"Drawing. Sketching, really. I illustrate books. Before that last year at TL I used to keep this to myself for fear of being called a sissy or something. By that year I had enough confidence so I didn't care. You used to speak of the wonder of nature, the mystery in a flower, the miracles of growth, and of our discovery of beauty."

" 'Flower in the crannied wall . . .' " the director quoted.

"Yes, that sort of thing. You quoted that bit more than once. I discovered where that came from, too. But you passed on to us, some of us, at any rate, something of your own search for understanding, for reality, the heart of things."

Anita spoke up. "You gave George his conviction of some kind of spiritual reality," she said simply. "Most people, our generation anyway, don't seem to have it, this definite feeling of something beyond the world of the senses. I mean, if they do admit there's something back of matter, nature, they don't care enough to bother."

George's face took on a far-away look. Suddenly he broke into his wife's thought. "I've got it now. It was this little verse that set me pondering:

> *Reason has moons, but moons not hers*
> *Lie mirrored on her sea,*
> *Confounding her astronomers,*
> *But O! delighting me.*

There are all sorts of signs, just as you said, and if you want to ponder them, they lead on to a completely different view of life.

"I do appreciate your speaking of all this, George. People don't find it easy to communicate on these levels. What kind of books are you illustrating?"

"I began with children's books. They're the best market, and a constant one. Not too many adult books use sketches. Just occasionally. We've had to change our life style to adjust to this. But I find some publishers come back. They say they see depth in my pictures, a suggestion of something beyond. Just recently I've started painting. Haven't sold anything yet, but I see people here and there stopping to study something I've tried to put into a painting. They'll want them after a while. Takes time."

As the director reflected on George's conversation he was struck by one aspect of it, the lack of any conventional religious reference, except for Malachi. George was typical of modern youth. There is often a veneer of bravado, of scorn for all forms and attitudes in any way associated with the Establishment. But beneath the rebellion, there is a deep hunger in many young people for some sort of non-material reality. A recent translation of the First Beatitude expresses this well: "Happy are those who recognize their spiritual need, for they shall see God." They shall achieve an understanding of Reality.

In our daily Meetings for Worship we try to start where people are.

These young people have a remarkable sensitivity to injustice, a smouldering indignation at long-standing inequities, at the shameful advantage the well-to-do, the comfortable, the "successful" take of the poor, the helpless, the disenfranchised. Slavery, they rightly remark, hasn't ended. It just takes more subtle forms.

In commenting on the passing scene one refers to the principles of love and courage and compassion and empathy stated and demonstrated by Jesus. But a speaker may refrain at first from tracing these principles back to their source. Later on, one can speak in passing of the young revolutionary who set the ancient world by its ears; who fought with courage and singleness of purpose for the better, saner, more compassionate society we dream of today.

In speaking of the secret longing within each of us, we can eventually state the psychological truth which is summarized in the famous words, "Ask and ye shall receive; seek and ye shall find; knock and it shall be opened unto you. For everyone that asketh receiveth, and he that seeketh findeth; and to him that knocketh it shall be opened."

Eventually in discussing approaches to meditation which the new generation has discovered in Zen Buddhism and other esoteric systems, one can cut through the wordiness and obscurity of some of these forms by quoting, "Enter into thy closet and shut thy door and pray to thy father which is in secret; and thy father which is in secret shall reward thee openly."

We have gained substantial ground, in fact, when we dare mention prayer at all, when we can put it in its proper perspective as communion with something deep within us, not just "begging for something from somebody who isn't there." We are ready to set forth a modern approach to religion which needn't outrage our reason, but just goes far beyond it. No need to regret the utter repudiation of formal religion. The ridiculous anthropomorphic, Establishment-serving deity *is* dead, and no loss. The wreckage of out-dated, out-moded forms must be cleared away. The danger is that in rejecting religion of that sort, youth may lose also the glimpses of truth the old forms embodied.

I hope it is not just unsupported optimism to think that the next generation will swing around to cherishing the truths hidden in some of the old forms, and to a rational reading of the greatest source of most of the psychological and spiritual truths we live by, the Bible. There is a natural appeal to youth in the figure of the young radical who condemned so openly the hypocrisies of his time, knowing well where his frankness would lead.

This longing of the human spirit for some kind of certainty beyond the material senses sometimes takes strange forms. The rituals of some of the smaller cults require patterns of total acceptance, or irrational belief far more stringent than those of the Christian religion, even though they may use the Bible for proof, of a sort, for assertions that often are irrelevant to the real business of living a full and abundant life. Do they satisfy some of the yearning for certainty for a fearful, uncomprehending mind? This may be. At any rate, a guru in coming to this country is never without his loyal, devoted following, no matter how strange the truths he wrests from the world's sacred books.

Better this, perhaps, than the blind credulity of some of the "Jesus freaks." A pair of them stopped in on their former camp director some time ago and precipitated an argument about the age of the world.

"The earth is forty-two hundred years old," one of them asserted confidently.

"Can you be sure of that? How do you know?"

"God told Moses so on the mountaintop."

"He said at that time that the earth was forty-two hundred years old?"

"Absolutely. You can read it yourself. It's in —"

"No, no. I'll take your word for it. But there's trouble here. Moses we can date from the plagues of Egypt and the strange behavior of the Red Sea in receding and then flooding back in what must have been a giant tidal wave. These phenomena correspond in a striking way with the blowing up of the volcano of which the Aegean island of Santorini is the half-moon remnant. Knossus perished at the same time. That was, roughly, 1500 B.C. Therefore the world must now be forty-two hundred plus fifteen hundred plus nineteen-hundred seventy-two or between seventy-five hundred and seventy-eight hundred years old. And this takes no account of irrefutable evidence of geological time, and evolutionary time, all of which substantiates a much more wondrous view of the earth than your view provides for."

They looked at their director blankly. Then one of them remarked gently, "Well, I don't know about all those things, but the world *is* forty-two hundred years old. The Bible says so."

Despite these reactionary whirlpools and eddies, youth by its very nature is optimistic. It is ready for a view of life which does not deny reason but goes beyond it, which does not accept blindly but arrives through science and reason at the point where faith begins. This will be an activist view of life, socially oriented, shot through with Christian hope. This hope, almost unique in Christianity, can ripen into belief, and belief into faith, although borrowing much from the truth in other religions: there are many paths up a mountain.

With faith comes a sense of purpose, and a happiness which has always characterized the mystics, Christian and non-Christian, great and small. Like the poor peasant woman in Voltaire's story of "Vishnu," one can be supremely happy without comprehending the sweep of infinity. The Brahmin priest who scorned her because he knew Vishnu didn't exist seems to have been pretty unhappy. Though youth would probably reject this, Augustine's famous remark can be applied to our present condition: "Our hearts are restless until they find repose in thee."

"Thee" may turn out to be no orthodox type of diety, perhaps nothing presently recognizable as God. No type of man-made, limited, partisan, remote concept can satisfy the sophisticated generation of the future. But limitless vistas beckon. Everything is possible.

Somewhere in Rufus Jones' voluminous writings he says in speaking of human potential illumined by the spirit, "Claim everything!" This is our rightful heritage as sons of God. But there is work to do on ourselves before we are in a position to enjoy this rich inheritance.

Such is the reasonable but tremendously exciting view of life campers and staff have heard at Timberlake. If it has rubbed off in some measure on even a few listeners, one should feel richly rewarded.

10

Canoe trip

The flotilla on the Upper Connecticut is noteworthy in several ways. The canoes keep together, not side by side in formation, but within hailing distance. Gear is distributed carefully through each boat for balance; knapsacks are lashed to the thwarts. Two of the four canoes have a passenger, reclining at ease on duffel bags, trailing a hand in the water until remonstrance from the stern brings it in. Unlike some of the similar fleets encountered on the River, there are no uniforms, unless you allow the application here of the line from the Camp song: "The only suit we like to wear is a deep-brown coat of tan."

But the striking thing about this group is their paddling. Each paddler seems perfectly relaxed; his stroke is effortless, yet the rhythm of the boat is never broken. Each prow surges forward powerfully as it responds to the strength in the stroke. The only paddler who seems conscious of his stroke is the thirteen-year-old in the prow of the first boat. A slender figure, with black hair and dark eyes that scan the shores restlesslly, he paddles with a certain stiffness hard to define. With the others it is as if they had paddled all their lives. This boy uses his paddle with a conscious precision which suggests a skill learned more recently.

And this is the case, for the boy is Larry Somers of the Explorers'

Club. The trip into the wonderland of Floating Island Cove had been just a bit scary at first for the boy from the southwest. The experience of looking far down into dim reaches below was very new. But it had also been an inspiration to Larry. He had worked morning and afternoon, and sometimes evenings, to get to go on one of the canoe trips. There was so much to learn. You had to be an expert distance swimmer as well as an able paddler. You had to be "drown-proof," that is, you had to master the rugged discipline in watermanship that equips one with the know-how to meet any kind of aquatic emergency. By dint of determination, and pestering water-front staff to give him extra help now and then, Larry had done all this. For the techniques of the campcraft which must be mastered also, Larry had good background. And despite the years of riding alone in the back country of Arizona, the boy had shown himself able to be a cooperative member of a group, taking his share of responsibility without having to have it pointed out to him.

There was only one way in which Larry was annoying — he always managed to leave his sneakers when they stopped for a swim from a sand bar.

"Why wear the things anyway?" his stern paddler asked him in disgust. "You'd think we were going to jump out of the boats on nails or glass instead of good soft sand."

"Yuh, but it's not always sand. Sometimes there's a rim of stones, and I don't want to be last one in and a rotten egg."

"So what if there are stones now and then? Anchur feet tough yet?"

After having to head the fleet back to a swimming spot because of the plaintive bleat set up by Larry when he discovered he didn't have his sneakers, the counselor in charge had taken to checking the shore for the Somers' shoes. Then he decided this was bad training for Larry, and that he'd have to learn, perhaps the hard way, to take care of his gear. Thus it happened on the way back downstream that Larry's sneakers were left reposing on a sand bar and when they returned to civilization Larry had to walk barefooted on the hot pavements of the river town where they left the canoes for the next trip.

But the trip was worth all the stress of preparation and lost gear. The River wound through woods and beside farmlands and around gracious hills. At times it was in sight of the road; more often a wide fringe of woods and fields gave the illusion of aloneness. The single-track railroad that paralleled the Vermont shore was companionable. The engineer on the dawn freight always tooted his whistle when a group sleeping on the sand bar waved to him in the dewy dawn. The fresh corn they arranged with a farmer along the way to pick and pop into the kettle was a long-to-be-remembered treat, as was the warm milk the old gentleman brought down to them that evening. He stayed to talk about crops and the difficulties of growing corn on a flood plain. It was another new world for most of the boys.

Then the lazy swim in the moonlight just before turning in. Watching the dying embers of the campfire and listening to the junior counselor's "two-sentence ghost story" that left one chuckling, and a bit uneasy, too. "No," said the rich American who had just bought the English castle, "this old pile is supposed to be haunted, but there's nothing more unreal than that gardener out there on the lawn trundling the wheelbarrow."

"Sir, there *is* no gardener out there trundling a wheelbarrow!"

It is, then, a select group that gets to go on one of the big trips on the waterways the Camps have explored. There are several inviting trips in the New York State six-thousand-acre Forest Reserve, but these are so far away and often so crowded that it has seemed better in recent years to spend approximately the same mileage and time to reach some of the unspoiled lake systems in Maine. One in the past has been Umbagog and its tributaries. Another is Asiscoos. The latter body of water is sometimes pretty badly infested with motorboats, but it is still a beautiful lake. Since "development" has started on one side of the lake, its canoeing seasons are numbered.

There are several good canoe trips right here in Vermont. The best, to judge from camper popularity, is Lake Somerset in the southern part of the state. For years the Camps have canoed these waters. This largest artificial lake in Vermont, created by what was for many years the largest earth dam in the country, is owned by the New England Power Company, which has kept its shores completely undeveloped. Beaver dams on the feeder streams, little coves where the pond lilies grow, islands for camping and for exploring, make this a fascinating trip under the leadership of a mature counselor who himself knows something about these natural wonders. After the Company had been forced to ban overnight camping on the shores of Somerset, the Farm and Wilderness Camps enjoyed camping privileges on the islands of the lake for several years, owing apparently to the endorsement of the caretaker who was willing to vouch for the careful camping practices of Farm and Wilderness groups. When the New England Power Company adopted a uniform policy of no overnight camping on any of its lakes and streams, the Camps made an arrangement with a conservationist group owning a tract of land near the lake to set up a camping site on their property. From here the Camps often arrange a "switcheroo." They bring down two canoeing groups. While one is enjoying the lake, the other is hiking the rugged shores and contiguous mountains.

It was one of these groups that the Somerset caretaker set out to visit early one morning. He came on them as they were holding Meeting for Worship. Coming up the knoll to the camp and seeing this cluster of youngsters sitting motionless in a circle with heads bowed, the man was mystified.

"God, that must be one helluva good crap game," he sang out in a loud voice as he came nearer.

Through the interest of several counselors, campers in recent years have had a taste of white-water canoeing. Exciting and challenging in itself, though no more challenging than one of the big Maine lakes in a wind, this taste has rather spoiled the older campers for the quiet pleasures of a simple canoe trip in calm water.

The Connecticut River, where it forms the boundary between New Hampshire and Vermont, has offered both types of trips. Some three decades ago when the river was relatively unpolluted, the sections between Wilder and the next upstream dam were much loved by older campers. There were favorite camping sites, sand bars for swimming, and a couple of island shelters along the way. As the river became more polluted, and it was no longer possible to swim in most of the area below McIndoe Falls, trips started going almost up to the Canadian border and shooting the rapids on the way down. But sometimes these rapids have so little water as to be extremely dangerous. At times and in some seasons the water can be so low as to make part of the course impossible. This is unnerving when encountered unexpectedly. It requires good judgment and firmness on the part of the counselor in charge, for some of the boys will regard this sort of water as simply an additional challenge of which some faint-hearted leader is determined to deprive them.

Over the years there have been spills in such water, involving skirmishes with mortal danger which have set Camp policy against such situations. At other times counselors have been faced with keeping a trip reasonably dry and happy in five days of constant rain. There have been trips on which, despite sound health and reasonable precautions, someone has been taken sick and has had to be rescued by a car sent up from Camp, effecting a difficult meeting with much delay.

But there have also been golden memories of perfect days spent swimming at favorite sand bars; of little streams explored when the canoes could scarcely make the tortuous turns as the watercourse wound its way through lush meadows and into shaded copses. There are memories of sumptuous meals produced by the waterside. One went swimming later to wash the dishes where the current swung near the shore.

Then there was that unforgettable trip during the Second World War when the Camps had no gas coupons for unessential travel like taking canoeists to the river. Travel had to be by public buses, with long waits at changes, and a carry of over a mile down through a town with all the gear and the boxes of food. But the effort was well worth it. For five magic days the group lived like Indians, paddling their sturdy craft up a wilderness stream, with an occasional bridge to recall the voyageurs to civilization. When the group reached the starting point again to turn over the canoes to the next group, the leader of the new group, kneeling to steady an incoming boat asked, "Have you heard the news?"

"No, what news?"

"Japan has surrendered."

A canoe trip is often more leisurely than a hike, and more flexible. One can take along more than on a hike, where everything must be transported on one's back, and where a certain shelter must be reached before nightfall, no matter what. On a canoe trip there is time to study with more singleminded attention the country one is passing through or the site where one camps. A canoe trip is a complete camp away from camp, a home away from home. Here your home is simple and puts first things first.

There will be time on a canoe trip to beach the boats and explore an interesting meadow or a small waterfall up a wooded glen. There is time for lazy discussion after the midday meal as one sits on a log or stretches out on a grassy shore to feast his eyes on the expanse of blue water before him. There is time in the evening for games, in and out of the water, and then for some reading aloud from a favorite story the leader or some camper will have brought along to share.

And always the learning goes on, learning to live together, learning how the complicated ecology of stream banks fits into that of the hinterland, finding out how to savor life with many of the pressures removed, and what the far reaches of the mind may reveal. The whole trip is a unique learning experience. It rates just about tops in fun and in profit. From the time the truck sets out for the river and the counselor in charge sees that his campers aren't selfish regarding the best locations for comfort and view, his teaching, if he is worthy of the name of educator, has begun. Mature, competent leadership, an essential particularly on a canoe trip, has set the spirit by the time the canoes are lined up on the shore, ready for shoving off. This spirit is thoughtful of everyone on the trip. It prevents bickering about partners and places in canoes. It calms excited voices and relaxes straining muscles so the fleet can swing over close by the shore to study a lush tangle of shrubs and vines.

"Can anybody figure out that fragrance ahead of us?" the counselor asks. "Must be a whole field of some plant in bloom. Sharp smell at first. then something sweet and cloying also. Anyone want to bet with me that milkweed is one part of it?"

Rounding the bend, the flotilla spots a rank growth of milkweed, with the faint fragrance of meadow rue along the water's edge. Birds are through nesting in these thickets, for it is August. Fledglings are learning to fly. To witness one such drama is worth a morning's paddle. Still another delight in skimming along close to shore is the occasional feasts of wild raspberries hanging out temptingly over the water in lush abundance.

A sandy spot along the shore means another swim. Who will be first over the side as the bows nose in against the shore? A beetling sand cliff rising sheer above the shore is scanned not only for bank swallow holes, but for possibilities of developing slides where the slope is not too precipitous.

Picking a spot for the night is always absorbing. Essential to camp, with permission of the owner, are just the right combination of meadowland or pasture, a forest edge for firewood, a clear brook or a spring nearby for pure water, and a place to beach the boats. If this is also a good spot for swimming, the location rates a triple A, and word of it is passed from trip to trip, along with a special mark on the well-worn map of the river.

For a group of impressionable youngsters a campfire, especially the one on the last night out, gets built into one's total personality for all time. The emotions of this occasion, the camaraderie of friends who have taken the rain with the sunshine, the rough with the smooth, all add up to blessing of mind and spirit to endure for life. Attitudes are not caught but sensed on this magic occasion. Who can know the new determinations taken at such a moment, to be called on years later in some time of stress?

The special satisfactions of this hour are not to be put into words. The canoe trip is itself the culmination of weeks of effort back at camp, crowning long hours of learning skills in campcraft, mastering water and canoeing techniques, safety training, and finding out the meaning of co-operation at a campsite. Small wonder that one is pleased with himself.

One particular trip has brought together an easy group of teenagers, among them that boy at the square dance early in the season, Jack Fox of the sturdy body and the tousled hair, the lad with the penchant for getting into trouble with the police back home. Jack, for once, is overwhelmed with the sheer magic of the night. There is something about the leaping flames of a campfire that stirs primitive memories. Water exerts the same spell. Here on this evening which climaxes the canoe trip the elements of fire, water, earth, and the star-studded sky combine to steady a venturesome, restless, impulsive, warmhearted youngster whose boundless energy is beginning to be directed by a dawning consciousness of what life can be. Through the trials and tribulations of a varied summer, the camp has put its mark on Jack. He is beginning to "wise up." By the vicissitudes of trying out authority and finding, sometimes painfully, the limits, but recognizing these bounds finally as reasonable, the boy has emerged as a different person, still restless and impulsive, but also at times thoughtful and reflective.

Here for instance at the campfire, after the songs and the stories, after the marshmallows are toasted over dying embers, there comes a moment of quiet. The cool of the August evening begins to invade the area of the fire; the sounds of night drift in. Waves lapping against the shore in the darkness tell of miles upon miles of river the crew has paddled over. As one looks up to the vast reaches of the sky, to stars that are worlds without number, the appalling magnitude of it all is suddenly overwhelming.

Not at all out of place is it for the counselor to open a pocket Testament and to begin reading quietly in the light of his flashlight one of the Psalms of wonder:

"When I consider thy heavens, the work of thy fingers;

The moon and the stars, which thou hast ordained;
What is man, that thou art mindful of him?
and the son of man, that visitest him?"

For Jack it was the prime teachable moment. His head was bowed in thought.

"That's right, what is man? And what am I? Something kind of wonderful and big, I guess, but also small, tiny. What's it all about? It can't be just this no-God stuff. Too complicated to just happen. Those stars, the waves, that baby bird the other day, Jim reading there, and the way he doesn't let you get away with a thing but still he's such a great guy. These other fellows here. It's great; it must have meaning. Someday I'll get it all figured out maybe."

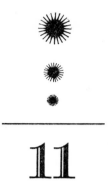

11

A sense of purpose

"So you're a high-school senior, Mark. When you were last at camp you were about fourteen. Right?"

"Yeah. In the Rangers." The tall boy smiled and his eyes looked into the distance.

"Life was simple then, wasn't it! What college you headed for?"

"That's just it: I don't know. Maybe I won't go to college, not right now anyway. No sense to it."

"Well, it's not a bad idea to take some time off to get your bearings. Any notion of what you want to do in life? Anything that appeals to you especially?"

"Can't say there is. Don't know what I want to do."

Mark swept a lock of unruly light hair from his eyes with long, slender fingers. They were intelligent eyes, and frank. In fact, the whole face bespoke sensitivity—and confusion. There was an air of deep uncertainty about the youngster, about his simplest movement, even the tentative way he brushed the hair back across his forehead. What a contrast to the self-assured, active twelve-year-old who had been so full of *joie de vivre*. Was it just adolescence that had extinguished this gaiety, or was there something else?

For one thing, Mark had begun to think; he had started to look around him, to observe shrewdly. What he saw he didn't like. He was typical of the upper-middle-class high-school youth we all know, sated with material comfort to such a degree that the satisfaction of a wish often came before the wish was clearly formulated. The old Horatio Alger motivation of the eager boy on the way up the economic ladder had no lure. Why should Mark want to make money, except to prove his independence? He had never known the bite of straitened circumstances. He had arrived. Like the little old lady in Boston, she was already there, so why should she travel?

But there had been the chance to look around, too much, perhaps, for his own good, at least from the short-range point of view. Kids of this generation can always spot a "phony." They hate the hypocrisy that conceals greed. Greed spawns wars, even dirtier wars than those fought to "make the world safe for democracy." Greed also makes people callous to injustice, insensitive to the racial and economic inequities which lead to the decay of cities, the growth of slums.

The Camps had really failed this kid, the director reflected sadly as the conversation went on. Like Peter Lessing on hard drugs, Mark had picked up the habit of questioning which the Camps had fostered. But he had failed to adopt the ideals which might have replaced what he had discovered was hollow.

Why had the ideal of reverence for all life, compassion for the victims of our economic system, not shaped in these boys, and others that came to mind, a purpose deeper and more satisfying to them than just making money? If business didn't attract Mark, and there was no reason why it should, why hadn't he caught any of the burning social concern that had sent a number of Farm and Wilderness "graduates" into social service of some type? Often these youngsters had given themselves, heart and soul, to some movement of social significance. This cause sometimes evoked such dedication that a boy or girl was caught up in this effort, and thus found himself, and happiness.

If not social service per se, why hadn't the ideal of simplicity, the challenge of subsistence living close to nature, become a gateway into the new areas of ecology and conservation? "The fields are white with harvest, but the laborers are few." And Don Oldenberg and Alice Field, both of them on LSD, why hadn't the Greek ideal of reverence for the body, its beauty, its strength, its complexity, why hadn't these ideals, so often voiced at Camp, kept them from the hedonistic abuses common to our culture? Well, the inspired wisdom of the greatest Reformer of all time had touched some. Others didn't make it. Like the seed scattered by the sower in the parable.

But have we done all we could? Are there ways in which we could make our ideals more articulate without preaching? For each new crop of campers we might explain more fully and from varying points of view, or with new approaches, the reasons for the types of action in which we invite everybody to get involved. Perhaps we can have more bull sessions on questions basic to our action here. Our physical fitness program, for instance, and our reasons for promoting the Fifth Freedom could be put in sharper focus. Maybe we can encourage somebody who is a seasoned exponent of organic farming to work with us a day, then in the evening talk with groups of campers and staff about the rationale of organic methods.

And perhaps the current events sessions on Monday evenings can be pointed up into more effective discussions, if we put some real time into it. These might lead to a couple of weekend seminars with some fine young workers from the Friends Service Committee or some other group. Perhaps in all these areas we could—yes, we *must*—try harder. It's really vital, literally a matter of life and death, to some youngster beset by the shifting patterns of Suburbia. Realizing the venality and the shrewdness of much of our advertising; considering the overriding materialism in which some children are brought up, it's small wonder that not all of them find their way through this alluring maze into sounder values. Probably this is our most important mission.

During this somber reverie, at the time only a series of intuitions flashing through the conversation with Mark, we had gone on to other things. But the theme of bafflement, uncertainty, frustration was never far away.

"Well, Mark, you may have heard me mention in the German *Wanderjahr* during some campfire story, the one about *Germelshausen*, perhaps. In Germany a century or more ago, young fellows took a year or so off before apprenticing themselves to some craftsman. They just wandered around the country, seeing new sights, thinking, trying to get as much light on the human predicament as they could before settling down.

The wander year was a recognition that anybody might need a year, maybe more, to think things through. The idea was, apparently, that when a fellow began to observe life, in depth, as they say, and with mature understanding, he would find it basically good, despite the hanky-panky and chicanery you can find everywhere. The superficial aspects may at times be sickening; but deep down beneath that, there's a level where it's sound and rich. Have you thought of getting a job somewhere and finding out how the other half lives? I mean, not just dishwashing for a meal or so, or to earn a few bucks, but staying with some sort of job long enough to get to know the people around you and their hangups? Perhaps you could plan to save up a little cash so you could be independent. Just an idea. Keep in touch anyway, and remember, the latchstring is always out."

—Poor kid, I wonder how I would have weathered the kind of distractions and temptations these youngsters have to meet. No right to be critical of them, anyway.

The magazines are full of studies of our "drifting" generation. Books are being written on the decay of the family. So many influences in our swiftly changing culture add up to utter confusion for the new generation. And cities are impoverished by the concentration of our national assets on ventures in destruction or on policing the world. Most of these cities fail to give their youth the intellectual and spiritual riches they should provide, just to justify their existence as cities.

Anyone who has marveled at the complete absorption of a child watching animals, especially small animals, will readily appreciate what our rootless, technological, urban culture is doing not only to the family as a unit, but particularly to its younger members, in depriving them of familiarity with livestock and with growing things. With their first feeling of independence these younger members of society tell us in no uncertain terms what they think of our artificial, dishonest, predatory culture. Our youngsters in increasing numbers, as they reach the age where they begin to reason, will have none of it. One of the types of protest against things as they are is alienation, noninvolvement, disorientation. The values in our materialistic, militaristic culture, they tell us, are phony. The country has become the victim of self-seeking, manipulative, callous political dishonesty.

How does an individual come by his values? What are the value assumptions which undergird motivation? And what can be done to forestall the apathy of many members of the new generation? This should truly be the first goal of the Camps, of any camps, now that both the church and our system of public education seem incapable of the task.

In May one year, when the camps were already filled to overflowing, a letter came from a camp parent. "Could you possibly find room for Sam and Betsy Goldstein at this late date? Matters have come to a head in the Goldstein family. The kids absolutely refuse to be dragged off to Europe to get 'culture.' What they want at their ages is to get their feet down in the dirt, to get muddy all over and nothing said, to be friends with simple, primitive things, to enjoy their birthright as children. Perhaps later when their intellectual and esthetic awareness is greater . . ."

Of course, sympathy at Camp for this pair of young rebels made room for Sam and Betsy. This is how the Camps get crowded each year!

It is the lure of simple, primitive things, the call of the wild, that give the Camps their zip and go. Their effort to be honest, their challenge to adolescent strength and stamina, their concern with the primeval requirements of living which have tested the strength of youth through countless generations—these qualities in the Camps' activities lead to full involvement, to total commitment, to an abiding love. The values children sense in the environment of these camps call forth their best. No need for a slick sales campaign to brainwash young people into this set of values. They are natural to youth. They are the stuff that life is made of, life as it should be: clean, vigorous, purposeful.

The rationale of this view of things lies in the fact that in living close to nature, in tune with the elements, "making" one's own living, a child is reliving the evolutionary cycle whence has come our strength. As with any domestic animal or plant, the closer you approximate the environment in which the organism evolved, the finer and stronger the specimen will be.

When man's basic environmental needs are satisfied, his intellectual and spiritual nature can develop in a wholesome, natural way to the fullness of a given individual's capacity. And if the total environment, including intellectual and spiritual elements, is stimulating, motivation will come as a natural consequence of having accepted, perhaps unconsciously, values of a different order from those of our urban culture.

Let's consider the Bishops again briefly, that farm family who worked their upland acres to the east of Plymouth Lake. The Bishops probably had little intellectual or esthetic life, and we would not want to share their existence for long. Yet the chances are that they were happy, busy, fulfilled individuals. Our pattern is more complex. It must provide for other aspects of life too, aspects which seem to flower most fully in a city. But in this post-technological age of the 1970's, middle-class youth longs, Antaeuslike, for contact with the good earth whence it sprang. Instinctively these youngsters search for values antithetical to those around them. The longing for simplicity, honesty, justice, "love"—rather diffuse at present, but embracing the victims of our economic system—this yearning becomes imperative. It takes the form at camp of living in cooperation rather than in competition with nature. It is thrilling to feel one is in a measure making one's own living, taking care of one's own wants, functioning at times and among the oldest campers, at a subsistence level. It is thrilling to dispense with anything that separates us from nature. There is a desire to be rid of the gadgetry, the unneeded, enervating luxuries Madison Avenue has persuaded us we must have. It's all rather inchoate at present, and deeply subversive.

When this salutary revolution in values is clearcut and articulate, one dares to hope that these new values will include some of the human qualities which have tended to be downgraded: unselfishness, self-discipline, gentleness, compassion, patience, understanding, as well as others which a less frenetic mode of life should engender. No problem of motivation here, absolutely none. The desire to pass on the new discovery, to persuade, to convince, sparks the deep impulse within us to share with others what we have found precious.

The problem of motivation is in the system, not in the new generation. Take the Goldstein family. When the dispute about Europe surfaced, Mrs. Goldstein consulted Sam's home-room teacher. The educator's reply was almost a copy of what Jack Fox's guidance counselor had told Mrs. Fox: "The boy has a good IQ, but he won't apply himself. He's like so many students today: no motivation. If we could only wake them up, they could really go places."

Although the teacher was so completely enmeshed in the System to Stifle the Impulse to Learn that the truth couldn't break through, Sam *had* waked up. That was the trouble with him, from the teacher's point of view. And he was going to go places, but not the places his parents and his teachers wanted him to go. With no ambition to be the man in the gray flannel suit, Sam had determined that he was going back to camp where he had found the realities that turned him on, the realities of sun and wind and rain, of a calf that licked your hand when you fed her, of rows of corn that would mean corn roasts later on; of mountains to climb that challenged young muscles, of subsistence training which tested knowledge of wilderness roots and plants, skills in fishing, archery, and snaring, if the vegetarian diet of wild plants and berries gave out. And there were new ways of relating to peers and elders in the close-knit community whose democracy was of his own making and preserving, his and others who recognized the opportunities for responsible self-govern-ment. As easily as night blended into day these opportunities led into effort, into achievement, into the glow of satisfaction with something important accomplished. They had a built-in motivation.

Why couldn't school be like this? Of course it could be; here and there it is already. But it will take a complete overturn of present educa-tional relationships. We have the cart before the horse. We try to feed students knowledge before they see any need for it. Perhaps there isn't any need for some of it, even for much of it. If education began with the realities of a boy's or girl's environment, be it city or country, it would tap an instinctive interest in exploring and understanding one's surround-ings. Thence one could range farther afield, eventually into the intellec-tual and the historical environment of the culture itself. Always this exploration must be active, must, if possible, be participatory. Admittedly this is easier in the country than in the city. If a school's "grand campus" can be the woods, the upland pastures, the wilderness, and those selec-tions out of the wilderness we call a farm, the setting is perfect. In a city one must work harder to make the experience of environment participa-tory, but it can be done. It is being done.

Not only Sam Goldstein's sister Betsy got caught up in the excitement of activities connected with the environment, activities which often modi-fied the immediate surroundings in some way, or satisfied deep longings for creativity. The comradship of peers at camp, the warmth and under-standing of dedicated adults, quickly soothed the ruffled feathers of rebellion. The girl settled in with the ease and satisfaction of one return-ing home after a too-long absence. Besides the same interests and respon-sibilities in farming and gardening and housekeeping which absorbed her brother at Timberlake, Betsy reveled in some which were distinctive of her own favorite camp. The discovery of design and beauty in nature led to efforts to transmute it into patterns in other media. Weaving and pot-tery and water colors offered challenges to self-expression. These were experiences different each year, offering a source of never-ending delight.

The joy of small group singing, a tradition at the Camp, was one of her happiest memories. It became a living experience again. And despite allegations to the contrary, some of the girls, like Betsy, turned out for the Monday evening joint current events sessions as much for the intellectual stimulus as to "be with the boys."

Special events such as Sunday afternoon concerts or homemade dramatics or a far-ranging discussion explored hidden areas of feeling of which Betsy had been only dimly aware. These all added a new dimension to doing things together.

Altogether a good life for a child, an adolescent, or an adult, with, of course, appropriate variations. Having time to know the married staff and to discuss, with just one or two friends, matters of deepest moment to unfolding minds — this was all like an ideal and extended family with everyone caring about everyone else. Perhaps this could even be a model for the Blessed Community of the future, when we can restrain the forces of evil in the world so there may be a future. This will be a part of the task of the new generation. In the effort, problems of values and motivation get solved. And even through some of these youngsters who are currently turned off from things as they are, one can justify the faith that there will be a future.

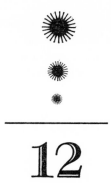

12

Democracy is listening

A visitor to one of the Camps remarked that he understood why there was so little friction. "Just watch the director talking to a kid before a meal when the gang is waiting for the signal that soup's on. You'd think that one boy was it. Nobody else there, no visitors, no key staff, just that one little boy trying to explain something that's bugging him. And the director's mostly *listening*."

True democracy must always be like that. It should be based on the ideal of reverence for life, the Quaker feeling for "that of God in every man," respect for another's point of view however it may be at variance with one's own. Sounds great on paper; in practice it's hard to achieve, and one's score is seldom perfect.

The simplest, and the most important unit of the camp democracy is the cabin group. Once a week, on regular schedule or when the spirit moves, the gang gets together to overhaul cabin chores or cabin relationships, or to make recommendations to the weekly Cabin Representatives Meeting. A director who sees the importance of these cabin meetings will set aside part of an evening regularly for them, and for other activities as a cabin group.

This is the occasion for which is built the little cabin fireplace in the adjacent woods. The cabin group has taken the time to rim the council-fire area with a circle made of short logs to sit on. A goodly supply of kindling and bigger wood will be stored under the cabin. Slender sticks for toasting marshmallows will probably be found on a shelf by the fire-wood.

The key to the success of such a gathering is the counselor. He sets the tone, he will know when a group is drifting off into trivia or when the meeting could degenerate into a gripe session. Skillful leadership will allow time for legitimate complaint while gently turning off the trivia.

The Catamount Cabin offers one of the best examples of these meetings. The Catamounters have been enjoying a cabin evening. They've had a quick game of frisbee, all hands involved, then a dip. Now the boys who have been privileged to lay the fire have done their job, helped by kibitzing from the part of the audience already seated on the logs. Eager flame, licking the dry kindling, beats back the deepening shadows. The last stragglers arrive on the double-quick, having finally located marshmallow sticks. Toasting these delicacies is the first order of business, with some argument about whether black is better than "a nice toasty brown."

When all have had their fill, or enough to hold them anyway, the musician of the cabin produces his harmonica and strikes up the lilting melody of "Road to the Isles" or the song about the poor guy that got lost on the MTA and was doomed to ride forever under the streets of Boston between Park Street and Scully Square. Someone knows most of the verses, all join enthusiastically on the chorus.

After the order of "Sweepers and Cleaners" for the cabin has been overhauled, the assembly gets down to major issues. Someone has suggested that not enough time is allowed for sports. What can we cut out to get more time? How about less campcraft? Just take it out on the trail and learn while you hike. "Yuh, but think of the new kids who don't have any campcraft skills. They could sure louse up a trip. Real killjoys. And they can't take their turns cooking at a central fire. Who wants to eat burned food?"

Fewer weekly sessions of work projects is suggested, but it develops that some guys like work projects a lot.

"It's my favorite vegetable," one boy remarks. So the decision is to instruct the Catamount representative to bring the matter up at the weekly cabin representatives' meeting. If the need for more sports time is a general feeling through the camp, perhaps something can be done, no agreement as to what.

The "Cabin Reps" had heard this one before in other years. A thorough canvass of camp activities failed to turn up any activity that a majority could agree might be cut down to give more time for sports.

"So we just ask at lunch how many want a game of soccer or whatever, and if there are enough, we go ahead and have it. All right?"

This solution, formulated by the clerk, was noted down by the recording clerk as something to be offered as a "policy" to the whole camp.

The all-camp meeting, council fire, or powwow, as it had been variously known, generally comes on Saturday evening. It may be combined with group singing, or a quick report on some trip, or a talent show, etc. It may be followed by a retelling of an exploit of Mad Morgan, or some other thriller. But in between, campers and staff will ponder the complexities of running the operation. A little discussion reveals to individuals that scheduling activities isn't so simple after all. In fact, it's real complexicated. The powwow had no better solution for the sports problem than the Cabin Reps had suggested. But everyone understood the program better.

But from the floor came an unexpected issue, that of hiking in the camps' own ample acreage where there was no question of enough wood for campfires, versus hiking the Long Trail, with increasing pressure to ban all campfires, requiring hikers to pack in camp stoves.

Several counselors groaned when this came up, for they knew the matter had been the subject of long discussion in the weekly meetings of the Advisory Council, a body made up of the directors of all the Farm and Wilderness Camps. The director of Timberlake, who had, of course, been a part of these discussions, reviewed briefly the thinking of the Council.

"I remember my own Camel's Hump trip. I'd hate to think that kids now can't get to go on a hike like this. Yet the overuse of parts of the Long Trail is going to require fewer Mansfield and Hump trips in the future. It's going to bear down on us soon, and we may as well face it. We should be glad more people are discovering nature, I suppose."

"If they don't destroy it instead," a junior counselor observed. "Overuse of park lands is a problem out West, too."

"In another year or two," the campcraft head remarked, "it's going to be a choice between spectacular views, then sitting around a gasoline stove at campfire time, or less spectacular views, but still good rugged hiking, much of it in our own wilderness, with all the wood we want. Which will it be?"

"Camel's Hump," several voices cried at once. "Campfires," another chorus countered. "The Hump"—"Campfires."

One of those quick near riots which can sweep a bunch of lively boys was prevented by the head of one of the three lodges. Jumping up quickly, he motioned for silence.

"We don't have to decide this now," he said quietly. "What I think may be worked out is a compromise. Each guy that's qualified gets to go on one Camel's Hump trip before he's outgrown the Camp. He'll go for the hike, the scenery, and not to enjoy a leisured trip of exploring the little byways we like to find. He'll do *that* on some of our own trails, new ones in the Saltash-Nineveh wilderness where we can build far-out campsites and trails through rugged country with views that will take your breath away. See, you've never known any of these spots," he added, noting the incredulous glances exchanged among friends.

"Chateaugay has lots of places for good campsites," an older boy contributed. "And there's some beaver ponds up there."

The issue wasn't settled, of course. But a lot of new campsites near home came to light. Everybody, it seemed, had his own favorite spot. And in the course of the discussion campers and staff began to realize how complicated it can be to set up policies true to basic values and yet mindful of the diverse feelings of smaller groups.

This matter of the Long Trail had been mentioned during a senior staff breakfast that very Sunday morning, which was why the Lodge head at the powwow had been able to speak up so quickly. These senior staff Sunday breakfasts, and junior staff suppers, were another part of the camp democracy. There is no agenda on these occasions, just a chance for good fellowship, and the opportunity to bring up anything that might be on a counselor's mind, including, sometimes, two or three youngsters whose behavior needs guidance from other observers.

After most of the senior staff has left the pancake feast, the Steering Committee stays on until time for Meeting for Worship. Consisting of the three lodge heads, plus the directors of campcraft, water-front, and projects, and the camp director himself, this little group tries to assess the feeling of the Camp and guide the general schedule of the next week to accommodate any special needs. They review the trips planned for the coming week, any special events. They work out solutions to problems to propose at the Sunday evening staff meetings.

These staff meetings of the whole counseling group — the Counselor Apprentices take over the cabins — are usually preceded or followed by lodge meetings. Almost never do boys in cabins which may not be covered by a "CA" take advantage. The staff can consider with some sense of leisure, and with much of the detail already handled by the earlier meetings, not only the state of the Camp but the general needs of the whole group of Farm and Wilderness Camps. Occasionally ideas, new perceptions on a general problem, start at some such staff meeting and are carried back to the next meeting of the Advisory Council, with which some degree of staff rapport will have been established during orientation week before the opening of the camps.

At the smaller camps, Tamarack Farm, with its sixty to sixty-five campers, and the Nineveh camps with their maximum of forty campers each, it is easy for staff to feel that they represent the ultimate in democracy. The staff meetings after the Sunday evening powwows can be short, for many current problems will have been aired and settled in the earlier general meeting of campers and staff.

At the last camper powwow of the season, reactions to the summer's program with a view to changes for next season, seem so valuable that some staff member takes informal "minutes." As with the postcamp staff sessions on the season, these ideas are carefully reviewed during the winter to incorporate any new ideas that seem good.

The final powwow of the 1969 season at Flying Cloud, the most primitive of the Farm and Wilderness Camps, offers a good illustration of how camper thinking can shape a camp's whole future.

There had been a vague malaise among the older braves all summer, something one couldn't quite put his finger on. Hints of it had come out at earlier meetings. In a couple of the older tipis it had surfaced after the boys snuggled down into their blankets and lay watching the embers burning low before they drifted off to sleep. By the end of the season this uneasiness had become articulate. At the final powwow it emerged quickly in the remarks of one of the oldest campers:

"We talk about living like Indians! Big deal! Then we find we can't live like Indians, not really, because, of course, we can't hunt our food. And we discover that to go on a good wilderness canoe trip, more than just cruising around Lake Nineveh, we have to get into one of these white man's monsters called a truck and get hauled to some far-off waterway. And I notice the Tuscororas got their fat fannies hauled way up to Camel's Hump, then brought back. So in a way we are just playing Indians, though it's not like some camps where you dress in a blanket and just hop around a campfire with a tomahawk. But I want to live *more* like Indians. Can't we?"

"Yeah," another brave spoke up. "We do a lot of riding around white man country dressed in white man's clothes to start some far-off hike. But we don't know the country right around us as Indians would."

"Right," another camper agreed. "I don't know all the kinds of roots and berries and plants we could find to eat right on our own mountain. The blueberries I know, because they come in fair-sized clearings and I've found most of the clearings. But how about the raspberries that hang heavy where a big tree falls? Just a few such spots I know."

"And the black ash for weaving baskets. I know just *one*, and we shouldn't cut that down. There must be others, if we made a real search. I want to make my own white-ash bow, but we're so busy being dragged off for distant hikes that we don't have the time to get really acquainted with the woods as Indians would know them. I have a feeling we're missing the riches around us, and that's bad."

There was a pause. Then a brave spoke who was usually silent. When he said anything, therefore, it was listened to.

"Perhaps we should not go anywhere we can't go on foot," he suggested. "We can really explore this Saltash range, and on over toward Chateaugay."

The boy who had brought up the subject now spoke again. "I think we could still get a good canoe trip," he offered. "It's sixty miles by trail to Stratton. If we travel light and get into good condition ranging around these trails here, we can make it down there in three days, then three days back, and five or six days on and around Stratton. This would be our Big Trip of the year, and we could do it all on our own."

"I'm willing to try it," one of the Tuscororas remarked. "With really light gear we could do it. We still take too much on trips."

There was a murmur of agreement.

"Another thing I know we can do," a new speaker observed, "is to bring in all our own food. No more wheels in camp. Let the old logging road wash out, fell a couple of trees across it, haul everything in ourselves, perhaps up the Nineveh trail, not on the road at all."

Thus was born Flying Cloud's "Great Leap Backward," which has lasted now several years with only minor grumbling. The gardens have increased in size; more use is made of wild berries. There's talk of raising the Camp's own broilers to solve the meat problem, but there is enough sentiment that this isn't really "Indian," not at any rate what Indian braves would do, to permit any consensus. The canoeing problem is still to be solved. Groups have hiked one way. It awaits some intrepid older group to demonstrate that the sixty-mile hike is possible without taking too much time out of camp. Once it's tried it may become a tradition, like a number of other exploits at Flying Cloud.

Like the refrigerator problem, for instance, which had often been discussed at powwows. Some of the staff, together with some former Flying Cloud braves, about twenty-five in all, came up one February day several years ago. The thermometer stood at ten below. From planks and boards stacked ready by the little pond, they built a rough icehouse. With the old-fashioned ice saws and markers and ice peevees they had borrowed from an old-time farmer, they filled the icehouse before the dark came on, packing the cakes in with sawdust stored beside the pile of lumber. The ice party is on the way to becoming a tradition, never again involving both building the icehouse and filling it.

Not all the grist of the weekly powwows at the camps leads to such changes, of course. Much of the debate turns on what kind of rotation should be set up for clearing tables and whether the benches should be washed too. But any idea gets consideration. If it seems reasonable (after older staff have pointed out difficulties), it is likely to appear in some form during the season or the next year.

This is one of the strengths of the Camps. Many people's ideas have been incorporated in one way or another. It makes for variety, it leads to effective solutions for recurrent problems, and it gives members of the group a sense of participation, even of proprietorship.

With all this frank and free discussion, somebody may ask, "How come the question of coeducation hasn't come up and been acted on?" It has come up, often, and it will be acted on when there is a clear consensus at the Camps. There is always too large a group which sees benefits in the separation of the sexes below the middle teens to justify risking the present successful patterns of separation with frequent association between boys and girls in square dances, parties, work projects, some hikes, and common endeavor of many kinds.

But democracy is served in this as in other camp issues. Meanwhile, the Camps maintain their belief in democracy, not only for the sense of participation and consequent proprietorship it gives campers and staff, but for the longer-range benefit to our country. We don't do much flag waving; in fact, we have never had a flag-raising and lowering ceremony in the Camps. We are often frankly critical of the government and particularly of its foreign policy. But we have faith that our working democracy at the Camps will help add to the concerned and active electorate willing to spend time on self-government at the community, regional, and national level. Thus we will avoid in the future some of the egregious errors which have brought this country and others with it to the verge of economic disaster. Determined use of democratic procedures, we are convinced, can lead to orderly change. Children who have the vision and experience of a more considerate family life, a more responsive community life, can build a nation surer of itself and its goals. Thus, indirectly, it all leads to the better world of the future.

Since attitudes seem to be catching, this pervasive feeling of reverence for life, that God is a living force, bears its fruit in every aspect of camp relationships. The cabin group is a good example. A mature counselor, one who is no longer absorbed in himself and his own problems, will be a good listener. Prime time is at night, as the campers are getting ready for bed. You will often find such a counselor sitting on a bunk chatting with a youngster who has just wriggled down into bed, or standing beside a boy in an upper bunk, listening to him. Sometimes the subject is one of wider interest than a personal problem. It may be some world-shaking problem like why kids don't scrape the dishes better when they take them out to the kitchen, or why the staff is so slow getting down to the water front for general swim. If a matter seems of general interest, others may offer their opinions, and the counselor has a full-fledged discussion on his hands. It may be still going on when the slow bell for quiet rings.

As with Betsy Goldstein, Betsy and her brother Sam were nothing if not articulate. In fact, their distraught mother, after yielding to the barrage of opposition to dragging the kids around Europe to get "culture," remarked that both of the younger Goldsteins took after their father, who was a trial lawyer. The children were at least "a trial"! In a cabin meeting at which Betsy first brought the matter up, the girl was aware that a couple of her cabin mates were very unhappy about the issue and Betsy's proposal for settling it. The matter didn't get to the Cabin Reps meeting at all, for the representative from Lorelei was unwilling to bring it up. So Betsy broached it herself at the weekly all-camp powwow, putting it as forcefully as she could.

"As everyone knows," she began, "we've had riding here at Indian Brook long after TL riding was closed out because of cost. And now I hear that if riding continues at IB there will have to be a special charge to everybody who rides. I want to know if this is true," Betsy concluded, turning toward the director, " 'cause if it is I've got an idea."

All eyes turned toward the director. "I hadn't intended to discuss this with the powwow till we'd had a chance to think it over more," the director said with just a touch of irritation. "But since Betsy's brought the matter up, it may be as well to get camper reaction before we discuss it further in staff meeting. Next year we are faced with closing out riding here too, or making a special charge for it, which would cut out all the scholarship campers. What do you girls think about it?"

There was a stunned silence. Then Betsy Goldstein spoke up again.

"I guess girls like horses more than boys do. My brother Sam says it's a girl's chance to boss around a big hulking male animal. Anyway, anybody here knows how much I love riding. I'm often the first down at the horse barn at six o'clock. And I just love to take care of a horse, yes, even to shoveling manure. It struck me this morning when I got down there and found Rachel Somers already there, that probably Rachel couldn't have the fun of all this next year if we had to pay extra for it. I decided I'd rather go without it myself than have Rachel cut out of it while I go on doing it, just because my folks could pay for it. It's a hard decision to make, I know, and for nobody harder than for me. But those of you who would be against closing out the riding, just think of some of the girls who wouldn't be able to afford riding. Could you enjoy it yourselves while these other girls couldn't? Could you ride past them and see the way they looked at you, and still enjoy it? I couldn't, so I vote to close out all riding next year if a charge has to be made for those who ride."

Silence again. Betsy expected her two cabin mates to speak up in disagreement, but they didn't. Someone asked what they would put in place of riding, and the director had some ideas, not quite as good as riding, but still exciting.

Swept along by the spell of Betsy's eloquence and the tender spot which it had touched, the girls voted with no dissent to close out riding if a special charge had to be made.

The director was jubilant. "Now you're sure, girls, that this is the way you want us to consider it. All sure? Then thank you, every one of you You've solved a problem we've seen coming but really hated to face. I never get over being amazed at how fine you are!"

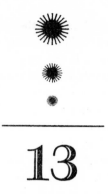

13

Camping from the neck up

Almost as delicate and unstable as democracy itself is the Monday evening current events session at Timberlake and Indian Brook. Like democracy, the success of the evening depends on able, concerned leadership and a goodly group of participants, the "electorate" in a democracy, who take an interest in issues and have gone to the trouble of informing themselves on at least some of the facts. With children one is working at the grass roots.

Some seasons we think that trying to generate this type of interest is too much to expect. Yet as we sense the concern among young people for fairness and sympathy, we are encouraged to believe that when more of the present generation of upper-middle-class youth get to the polls there may be a chance for honest government based on justice and compassion.

The format of Monday evening is simple. Half a dozen youngsters will have volunteered to cover one each of some six or seven types of news: national, foreign, ecological, scientific, sports, etc. A couple of other categories or subcategories may appear, depending on individual interests and the news itself.

Sunday afternoon, after rest-hour letters are done, the counselors in charge of current events at Timberlake and Indian Brook will get the two groups of volunteer reporters together to pore over *The New York Times, Time, Newsweek,* etc. The reading and discussion may go on through most of the afternoon. If the two counselors are knowledgeable in public affairs, the participants will feel compensated for missing out on Sunday afternoon cabin hikes or whatever else may be the activity. Farm and Wilderness cider and cookies to top off the occasion helps, too.

Monday, during rest hour, the two counselors work with their respective groups (not more than three, at most four, at each camp). Each "expert" runs over the material he plans for his three-minute report that evening. Other members of the group may ask the reporter questions on the background of his report, not trick questions, but honest queries for information. This, too, can be a rewarding session.

Some of those Monday evening sessions are memorable. Immediately after supper that evening little groups of Timberlake campers start up the road. These sessions are usually held in the lower lodge at Indian Brook, or, if the evening is quiet, out on the wide lawn by the water front, with the lodge handy in case of rain. By seven-fifteen if the leaders are on the job, the meeting gets started. One or the other of the two counselors in charge may make an introductory remark or two, setting forth the order of the reports, then introduce the young speakers in turn. It is considered exceedingly bad form to read from a manuscript or — unspeakable — to read more than a brief quote from a news article. Delivery should be simple, clearly spoken, and direct, with usually not even notes as a separation between speaker and audience. (This is excellent training, by the way, in public speaking, and is so recognized by some of the participants.) One or two quick questions are allowed after each speaker has finished, but long comments, objections, or anything argumentative is saved for the free-for-all at the end of the reports.

In camps like the Farm and Wilderness Camps, with diversity of enrollment, interesting and illuminating divergences in values may come to light, as for instance when a boy from the inner city, reporting on the "purchase" of a ball player by another club, remarked that the player was given a bonus of sixteen thousand dollars. "Sixteen thousand dollars," the boy repeated, rolling his eyes upward and speaking in awed tones. The upper-middle-class audience burst into laughter.

The second part of the evening may be just a few minutes, or it may stretch to half an hour. This is the free-for-all, a lively, far-ranging discussion sparked, if need be, by an adroit question from a staff member.

When most of the audience who want to say something have had their chance, the climax of the evening comes. Somebody in the camper or the staff group who has something to offer on an item prominent in the news will be asked to share his special knowledge or his concern.

Again it was a Goldstein who talked a whole meeting into accepting his point of view and his suggestion of a solution.

"My father gets a flier from the American Friends Service Committee," Sammy began when the counselor in charge of the joint current-events session asked if there was anything anyone would like to bring up. "This flier often has stuff in it that misses the newspapers. Like a report on political prisoners Thieu is holding in terrible jails throughout South Vietnam. These people are jailed without trial. Often they are tortured. And their only crime may be just that of disagreeing with the Government in its war policy or even just knowing somebody who disagrees and may be in hiding. Or even he may just have somebody on the inside who dislikes him and denounces him to the police. There's no democracy there, and no chance for public opinion to be heard. They just snuff it out. And this is the kind of government we as Americans are supporting. If it weren't for our money, everybody says the Thieu government would fall in ten minutes. Do we want to be responsible for things like this, snuffing out everybody that has the guts to speak up on something that he feels is wrong?"

"What can kids like us do about it?" somebody asked. "Who cares what we think?"

For the first time the counselor who was moderator spoke up. "I wouldn't be too sure about that. You guys, and gals, are the voters of a few years hence. If you feel deeply enough about an issue to go to some trouble to make your views known, it's likely that some legislator will be impressed."

There was silence. "We could write letters to our Congressmen," somebody suggested.

"No good. They're on vacation."

"But letters sent to their offices in Washington would get forwarded."

"Aren't there any Congressmen from Vermont?" somebody else asked.

"Sure there are. Must be two Senators anyway."

"Two Senators and a Member of the House," the moderator said.

"Where do they live?" somebody else asked.

"Where do they live, Steve?" the moderator asked. "You're a Vermonter."

"Well, two of them live within an afternoon's drive of Camp."

"Could we go see them?" Sammy asked eagerly.

"I will." "I will." "I will," a dozen voices spoke at once.

"Now wait a minute," the moderator cautioned. "What are you willing to give up to do this? A trip? A Saturday afternoon game? A favorite work project? A hot afternoon at the water front in order to be swaddled up in clothes and stuffed into a car. Think of the thing you'd hate most to miss, then raise your hand if you'd be willing to miss it to see our Vermont Senators, if we can arrange a time."

Two hands went up at once, two Goldsteins. Slowly a half-dozen more hands came up. The owners had thought it through. They were indignant enough about an injustice Americans are responsible for to be willing to forego their most cherished camp activity on the chance that such action might make some impression.

Others promised to write their own representatives and to try to work out a trip to see them if that should prove feasible. Thus the current events sessions can result in more than "talk," as important as that can be.

Occasionally the format of the current events evening is varied to permit some knowledgeable outside speaker. Then the camper reports are limited to the first half hour and the meeting is turned over to the guest speaker. From time to time there will be a panel of older campers and/or staff to discuss an important aspect of the week's news.

The most memorable evenings have been those in which some beloved counselor from a minority group has been persuaded to speak frankly on the point of view of his group. For several years a popular Japanese counselor had attended the sessions and refused to let himself be drawn out on the Japanese view of American policy. Then one evening he let go. What most of the audience had regarded as typical American generosity to a defeated enemy began to be revealed as a bid for power in East Asia, with not too much regard for sensibilities of the Japanese themselves.

An American black who had grown up at camp was finally moved to outline grievances of his race. When he had finished, these sensitive youngsters, who had only dimly suspected or heard intellectually, were overwhelmed by the scathing indictment of our long-standing and still continuing injustices to our black citizens.

"We have heard all this," one boy commented on the way home through the gathering darkness. "I've read about it. But here is Akki that we know and love saying this himself. I guess it's all true."

And again, an American Indian, daughter of a beloved Indian counselor killed in a military plane accident, pulled aside the curtain of graciousness which was her usual personality, and disclosed an ugly depth of resentment, almost hatred, of missionaries, past and present, to her people. These missionaries she said, had no understanding of Indian culture, nor did they *want* to see anything fine about it. They were bent on stamping it out to substitute their own misunderstanding of Christianity. They succeeded in robbing the Indian of his culture, his self-respect, his purpose in life; they substituted — nothing. Just a self-seeking, ignorant debasement of the religion Jesus stood for, just welfare, poverty, and dependence. The white man's history is a series of broken promises to the Indians, bad faith, treaties ignored. Her ancestors had died brokenhearted, still clinging to the belief that one's word is sacred, whether given in writing or just orally.

Such words from people one knows and loves are deeply moving, confusing at first, until one's further search begins to give perspective. Then it can be even more moving, as it begins to crystalize a determination to do what one can to right some of these ancient wrongs.

Only part of the homeward trek in the gathering dusk is devoted to impressions of the other sex encountered before and after the session. As devastatingly frank as the comments on favored or rejected members of the opposite sex are the remarks on the reactions to the stirring revelations of the white man's predatory role in history, a role still going on at the present time. An outsider, joining this thoughtful crew as they trudge along the dust of the camp road, might get the idea that here is a bunch of young anarchists, disillusioned with all government. Perhaps they are communists. This seems even worse, despite the demonstration in Vietnam that democracy in a group uneducated to its exacting demands disintegrates into flagrant corruption and dictatorship.

These perplexing questions and others lead the Senior Lodge, and occasionally the Big Lodge, to seize the first rainy evening after such a stirring session for a meeting of the Tauroboloi, the bull-throwers. The hearth fire flames high in the old lodge, kids bringing blankets sprawl out on the floor and crowd the benches along the walls. The head of the Lodge outlines briefly some question that's been talked about since the previous Monday night, and they're off. The only light may be that of the flaring flames on the hearth, fed by willing fire-tenders, while the rain beats a tattoo on the roof. After some discussion of our country's use of napalm to destroy people, defoliants to ruin the forests, bombs to make a desolation of towns, and to render the farmland unusable for generations; after a mention of the massacres, the reliance by the military on fiendish electronic weapons, some boy will remark:

"I still love what the flag stood for when it was adopted; but as of now, that decal in my brother's car when he came to visit seems to me right. It had the field of stars replaced by the word *Kill*. At least it's honest."

After this, a pause. "Well, we've got it," another boy remarked quietly. "It's our country. We'll have to live with it. We can try to change it. Try to convince kids at school, read up on economics, be ready to swing into action when we get older."

"But how? Revolution? Overturn everything?"

"Sure! It's too rotten to save. Everybody's a phony."

Over several assenting voices the lodge scholar spoke up:

"Have you guys read anything about the French Revolution? Yeah, and it happened in the Russian Revolution, too. When they got rid of the rulers, a demagogue seized power, and the result was worse than what had been destroyed."

"Perhaps Sweden offers some ideas, and the rest of Scandinavia, and socialism in England," a counselor offered.

"Let's hear about it, Jim," a voice called out. "My father's got that book, *Sweden, the Middle Way*. I should have read it."

That part of the discussion ended on the upbeat of hopefulness: the System wasn't entirely wrong. It had produced more abundance than any other for more people, even though this was partly by using up unparalleled natural resources. The trick would be to change the orientation of capitalism from making property its chief value to emphasizing the rights of people. This was complicated, and would take a lot of study and know-how. "But it's people like us who realize there's a problem and want to help that can do it," somebody summed it up.

There are other questions needing consideration. A boy from a school in which the student council had searched unsuccessfully for a convincing answer to the question of "Why shouldn't I cheat on a test if I get a chance?" was still wrestling with the issue.

Another time the goals in life are involved. "What's wrong with setting out to make a million dollars, so long as you don't do anything illegal?"

Somebody else had been disturbed by a remark in a morning Meeting for Worship. "Should we go along with this 'My brother's keeper' bit? I don't see it."

In the course of another discussion the matter of brainwashing was brought up.

"Isn't it the worst type of brainwashing when the military takes in a bunch of rookies and gets them to be willing to bayonet other guys their own age, the 'enemy'? They even get them to think they may have to heave bombs where they may kill women or children. Just too bad civilians got in the way. I think a lot of people go along with that."

And again, that hardy perennial: "How far should a guy go with a girl when he has the chance. Why not the full way, now that there's the Pill?"

In a free-wheeling discussion which can be properly termed a bull session, sooner or later, since sex looms so large in the thinking of any adolescent, the subject of boy-girl relationships gets an overhauling. It's not the what-ness of sex relations these kids are eager to learn about. It's the whethers and the why-nots that torment them. Books are too preachy. Their parents have a vested interest. Even their peers they suspect don't level with them: too interested in appearing to be Big Stuff. So trusted counselors are listened to eagerly, guys who won't give you a sermon but just the pros and cons as they see them. It can be a mind-stretching experience.

When a young adult leader can set the tone of complete honesty and matter-of-fact casualness, these youngsters will open up and speak with utter frankness, and that is pretty frank. Sometimes somebody will point out that the Lodge discussion is of necessity one-sided, for the reactions of the other sex are not represented. This may lead to an invitation to the same Lodge of Indian Brook. Youngsters usually come away from these joint discussions thoughtfully. "Gee, it gets complicated!"

There is no doubt that youngsters of the present generation want to be fair to the other sex, want to understand the ramifications, want to be able in the future to enjoy the full ecstacy of the sex act at its best. While they are determined to have sex without guilt, they are also willing, when such considerations are pointed out, to concede that responsibility, respect, and even reverence are pretty important components, as a favorite modern statement of the British Friends has pointed out.

The title of this chapter, "Camping from the Neck Up," is borrowed from an old friend of the Farm and Wilderness Camps, George Jonas, founder and director of Camp Rising Sun.

"Just because the summer lends itself so well to physical activity like swimming and hiking, work projects, games, we still shouldn't forget that man has a mind, too, and it needs its own fuel."

Camping offers other types of intellectual food besides current events sessions and the Tauroboloi. Reading aloud during rest hour is a long-established custom at Timberlake stemming from the time when Wakio, beloved Indian counselor, used to read from Ernest Thompson Seton's *Two Little Savages.* Now of a summer afternoon, if one goes down through the "Tipi Stadium" he is likely to see a group of youngsters sprawled out on the grass, some in the shade, some in the sun, listening enthralled to a chapter from *My Side of the Mountain,* or John Buchan's old masterpiece, *Prester John,* or Armstrong Sperry's *Call It Courage.* Possibly in one of the older cabins, at about this time, he may hear some boy reading from the *Grapes of Wrath, Catcher in the Rye,* or whatever the current favorite may be in adult literature.

An all-camp council fire which includes the weekly powwow to go over the recommendations of the Cabin Representatives Meeting will also offer chance for esthetic and intellectual enjoyment. There may be several items of classical music produced by a solo violin or flute. Later in the season, when the music lovers have had time to get together, there may be duets or trios, or even occasionally a quartet. The girls at Indian Brook often have a recorder group of perhaps a dozen players. They run more to vocal music, however. Several times during the season they will put on a far-ranging concert with catchy numbers which sing themselves again in one's ears as he walks thoughtfully homeward.

But the campfire on a trip, when a small group draws close around the flaming wood and faces are alight with the good cheer of a full meal and rollicking songs, offers a prime opportunity for mind-stretching. Some young cynic is sure to ask, if the two leaders are people boys respect and trust, "Jim, why do you want to be a surgeon? I understand they all get rich. Is that it?"

Jim pokes the fire thoughtfully during the ensuing silence. "Well, now that you put it that way, motives are mixed, I guess, and I can't *swear* that money doesn't enter in. But it's not the real reason, I'm pretty sure. I've seen my father save lives, people who were going to die of cancer, and he gave them years more of useful living. I've seen him restore a mother to a family that needed her, and relieve a poor guy of pain that was making life itself an agony. And I've got the same kind of mind, and the same hands. Tad said the other day they were a musician's hands, remember? I think a guy has to find out what his talents are, his assets of one kind or another, and choose the calling that satisfies the deepest drives. Then he can give other talents scope through hobbies. So that's my reason, or reasons. The money's incidental. Perhaps I'll give it all away to Common Cause, or Population Control."

The fire burned low while the little group thought over this honest statement.

"Guess that's another reason you got to understand yourself," Dan, the other counselor, remarked finally. "Didn't the Greeks have a word for it? Something carved above the doorway of a temple? 'Man, know yourself,' or something like that?"

Not only do the intellectual and spiritual aspects of the Camps help youngsters decide on careers, but they become a guide to thinking through the grievous issues of war and peace with which recent generations of young men have been faced. Like many other Quakers, the director has been asked repeatedly to vouch to some draft board for the honesty of a young man's concientious objection to war. Some draft boards are thoughtful enough to inquire into the other influences in a youngster's life besides his parents and his church, if any, which can shape his thinking. Here is one such response to a draft board:

Local Draft Board No. ————

Dear Friends:

———— ———— has asked me to give you some idea of the type of thinking he has been exposed to at Camp during five of his most impressionable years.

To begin with, these are Quaker camps, based on a thorough-going application of the Quaker Testimonies, which we consider to be just the Christian testimonies made explicit. We believe that religion must relate to life, to the everyday routine of a social group, or of a country. If these principles fail, or are not adhered to in time of stress, then religion is worthless, salt that has lost its savor.

Our day begins with a short Meeting for Worship, which may be a silent seeking together for the light to guide us through the day. Sometimes the Meeting is entirely silent; sometimes a participant may be moved to share some insight into the moral principles that must undergird our lives together. This often stimulates further sharing, and the whole experience may be deeply religious in the best sense. At any rate, this type of experience seems to make an imprssion on many who come here, both Friends and non-Friends.

We never make any effort to proselyte, convince, or convert, but we try to let what light we may have so shine that others may see how a social group may be soundly based on love and understanding, and on cooperation rather than friction and disputation; to realize that what does occur may be resolved by the fuller application of Christian principles. If one starts applying Christian principles to disputes, it is but a small step to the realization that international disputes could respond to the same type of good-will; that in fact, any other approach is a betrayal of the deeply religious principles on which our country was founded, and should make a person ponder deeply, and honestly, the probable un-Christian hidden motives which have occasioned the dispute.

Hence it is no surprise to us that ——— ————, who has through his most formative summers been part of life in this sort of group should come to feel that the application of violence to international affairs is repugnant to his whole being. Judging from the response of a number of other of our boys who have grown up in the Camps, and from what I remember of ——— himself, I would say that his position on the issues of war and peace is a completely sincere and honest one.

It is the need to write numerous letters of this sort which convinces us that an active and, in fact, effective intellectual life continues in the midst of all the allurements to physical activity at Camp. "Camping from the neck up" goes on as vigorously as any other activity.

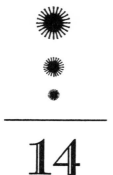

14

On being taken down to grow up

The charge that our school system prolongs the dependence of childhood, ignores adolescence, and withholds the responsibilities of adulthood is borne out by the increasing violence of street gangs, the use of alcohol and other drugs, and the psychotic personalities that have, by assassination, deprived the nation of at least three of its greatest leaders. To assume that all this malaise of the culture is attributable to faulty education alone is no doubt an oversimplification. But in contrast with the past, before public education became obligatory, we read of farm boys taking on what seems like an impossible work load, young aristocrats assuming command of men at sixteen or eighteen, of seafaring families whose sons captained their own ships at twenty.

So fully has this delayed adulthood become a part of our thinking that when a group of old-time camp directors get together to discuss their perennial problem of "how to hold the older boys," they often come up with just more intercamp tennis matches, a baseball league with higher stakes, or more parties between brother and sister camps. Such a conclusion misses the whole temper of the times. The broken windows, the overturned cars, the flagrant shoplifting indicate a need for vigorous action with the spice of danger, a craving for challenge, for action wtih a purpose, for responsibility. The Civilian Conservation Corps of Roosevelt, Tugwell and Wallace was an inspired answer to a problem which still cries out for attention here in the nineteen seventies.

The objection that kids nowadays don't want responsibility, that they avoid involvement of any kind, begs the question. Responsibilities suited to the age of a child must begin early. By the time most educators think of offering practical things for youngsters to do, their responses are already dulled by too many years of separation from all that could be meaningful. To provide this sort of individual education for the crowded schools of modern cities is an impossibility until the public reconsiders its priorities, until it spends more on the future of its children than it does on alcohol and tobacco. Meanwhile, summer camps at their best can serve as a corrective in some small degree to this shocking situation. But even with the simplest buildings, or no buildings at all, the growth of such camps is slowed by the lack of leadership, a problem the Farm and Wilderness Camps have long considered of highest priority.

Certainly for Jack Fox Timberlake's challenge to muscle and skill, its demand for involvement, the spice of danger inherent in many of the Senior Lodge's activities, brought forth in the boy abilities and strengths he had scarcely known he had. The lure of the Outward Bound camps for youth somewhat older is understandable. These camps demand that one put forth somewhat more than he ever realized he could. The resultant growth in self-esteem remains their greatest single benefit.

For Jack, who had built himslf a shell of swagger to conceal a deep sense of inadequacy, the first impact of the camp elicited a reaction of supercilious scorn. He hadn't wanted to come to one of those expensive baby-sitting agencies anyway. He would rather save the money toward a motorcycle. The many ways in which the Camp exacted an honest involvement led to rebellion. Understanding of the boy by several mature counselors got him through this stage with no confrontations. A quiet but firm effort to cut him down to size—he was "too big for his pants," as Gordie put it to his junior counselor—was combined with an appeal to Jack's physical prowess.

"Jack, old boy, you've got the broad shoulders and the brawn to handle the crowbar and pry out this stone. See, I've got it moving. Here, take my work gloves."

This was the work-crew leader's early-season approach to Jack's problem. After all, he did have good muscle. There was no harm in letting the guys see that. Then when the rock was out, the kid who was crew leader asked him to bring himself and his pry bar over to where some strength was needed again. By that time he was part of the gang. He was "hooked." It wasn't long after Jack's thus joining up with the path crew, that his degree of involvement could stand the lonely bout with the row of corn in the witch-grass. Such determination was possible because of a growing loyalty to a fine cabin leader, Gordie Brown, and the response of an essentially wholesome youngster to the clean, vigorous life of the Camp.

The completion of Jack's achievement of a mature self-esteem came about through a situation at Tamarack Farm. A canoe trip scheduled for late-season week on Assiscoos in Maine was jeopardized by the inability of participants to go. Did they have anybody strong enough and an expert enough paddler to fill in? One of the suggested candidates was Jack. From the point of view of competence, Jack qualified. He had shown himself a strong and skillful canoeist, picking up new techniques quickly. On a trip he always did his share. Jack was also more steady than early in the season. He had begun to think some of those long, long thoughts which are supposed to be the prerogative of youth. Instead of rejecting forthwith the Camp's special brand of spiritual awareness, he began, in some of the quiet moments which even an activitist has to accept during daily Meeting for Worship, to wonder whether there might be something in all this garbage about God. Not the way the old folks had it, of course, but something streamlined and bigger, nearer, and more mixed up with life and living.

All this made the boy at times willing to listen. "This trip could be the beginning of wisdom," Gordie remarked to his junior counselor. "Only wisdom is hardly a term you think of with Jack Fox." They both chuckled, for they liked the boy.

So Jack found himself bouncing along in the Big Green, the camp truck, on the long trip to Assiscoos.

The leader of the trip was a young woman, a project counselor from the farm. Her assistant was a man from the water-front staff. Jack wasn't sure he liked this setup. There were girls along too, for Tamarack Farm was a coed camp, but this was a different breed of girls from what he had known. He soon found that they could swing a canoe over their shoulders and hike along with it about as well as a boy, and as for paddling, well, what they may have lacked in brute strength they made up in skill and steadiness. No silliness about these girls, either. When the flotilla came to a good beach—Assiscoos was mostly uninhabited—they stripped off as quick as the boys and popped into the water. Then they sat on the shore and chatted while they dried off in the sun. No nonsense either, just matter of fact.

One of Jack's unhappy memories of the trip—there were several such—was that of a morning when they misjudged the sky and the wind. The sky looked bad, but it seemed to be lighter in the east, and there wasn't much of a wind. Nearly everyone but the counselor in charge was eager to be off. The counselor, who had the real responsibility, was doubtful about those clouds. Did it mean a big blow on the way?

"Heck, no," Jack volunteered. He was feeling his oats now. "It's looked like that every morning. Then it clears." The others supported him.

Despite the counselor's objection that this looked somehow different to her, the group, including her staff assistant, persuaded her to take off. For the first three hours it was fine, though they were getting a little tired from bucking the wind. But this proved to be the calm before the storm. The sky darkened, the wind freshened. The woman in charge of the group called out to keep closer together, within easy speaking distance, and head diagonally across to a point of land beyond them. Her voice was clear, but there was a no-fooling sound in it that Jack noted uneasily.

"We've got to make that point: nothing but rocks this side of it."

"Anything better beyond?" Jack heard someone call over to her.

"Not sure," was part of the reply. The rest was lost in the wind.

Jack and his bow paddler, one of the girls, became too busy for more conversation. As the boy allowed himself a swift glance ahead he realized the seriousness of their predicament. The waves were churned to frothing whitecaps. The wind tore pieces of this froth away and sent them splashing against Jack's tanned chest. It was too cold for comfort. And the boat had taken on an unpleasant roll. Jack sighted apprehensively ahead at the diagonal course they would have to maintain against the mounting waves. He dug in harder, with another glance at his bow partner's steady stroke. She was O.K. If she hadn't been, they could have swerved any time into a trough. This would have meant instant swamping. Where were the other four boats? They were all in sight, close ahead. Were they making any progress, or just keeping from being blown back?

The girl gave a swift glance over her shoulder. "Give it all you got,

Big Boy," she shouted through the wind. "Leetle more muscle. We gotta keep up with the others."

Jack dug in harder with his paddle, using energy he didn't know he had. He matched her long steady stroke, and with such strength that he wondered would the paddle snap. His arms began to ache. More speed, more speed. Forget the ache. More muscle. Their boat gradually drew up alongside the fourth boat. The third was just to port of it. Nobody looked out of his boat now. They were all struggling against the rising wind. When would the rain come? Could they make the point? It was a little nearer. There was a lone tree, a spruce, on the end of it. If they could make that tree! The waves hissed over the gunwales now and then like snakes writhing. The boat was awash. Lucky the duffel was lashed to the thwarts. His neck muscles began to ache. He tried to shift his fanny on the seat, but didn't dare for fear of missing the stroke. In spite of the vigorous exercise, he was cold, and soaking wet.

"Stroke," the girl called out. "Stroke."

He bent to the paddle again. If he didn't do his share they might really swamp. That pine tree was a little nearer. But the others were still ahead. They'd dropped back to last, but they weren't trailing by much. Got to keep it up, up, up. A numb sort of rhythm came to him and he fell into it mechanically: dig, up, in, dig. The tree *was* nearer. Two branches low down. But could he keep it up? He must. He had to. He must. He could see the waves lashing the point. Then the point disappeared—in rain. Sheets of it. Hail? It stung his shoulders. Stroke, stroke. He could *hear* the waves now crashing on the point. There it was. Stroke. First boat was rounding it now. Gotta keep well out, else the wind—He paused just the fraction of a second to true his course. The girl turned her head, slightly, as if to say, "Don't take it close, but—" They were rounding it, the point, that pine. There ahead of them—the rain was slacking off—they could see the first boat, *making for a sandy shore*. It was just a tiny beach between two rocky crags, but—shore. Don't slack now. Come in full steam. Last, but not by much. No rain now. Was the wind dying? Stroke. Second boat was landing.

Somehow they all made it. Jack's teeth were chattering. Fright? No, cold. He clamped his jaws together. When the so-welcome sound of the prow against sand came, pride made them seize the gunwale on opposite sides and carry the craft up, water and all, till it was out of the reach of waves. Then they sank down on the wet sand, exhausted, chests heaving, too tired for words.

"That was a close one," the head counselor remarked finally. "Next time we'll be sure. Storm's about over, I'd say. Let's see about some shelter."

His bow partner turned to him. "Good paddling, Big Boy. You got power."

Jack felt good all over, even though he knew the rest had kept ahead of him. He should have complimented the girl on her own difficult job of keeping the prow on the course, but he wasn't good at compliments.

Tents up, they crawled into dry sleeping bags for a little shut-eye, reviving in time to get supper. The weather had cleared. The waves were lapping on the shore with no touch of their earlier savagery.

After supper, the gang sat thoughtfully around the campfire. Nobody said much, probably all feeling guilty, as Jack was, for having persuaded their leader against her judgment.

"Well, anyhow," Jack remarked, in an ill-advised effort to play down the danger they had been through, and his part in getting them into it, "anyway, it couldn't have been as bad as what the boys of the summer canoe trip of the Cathedral Boys' School of Winnepeg had to buck last year. They were on a big lake, lots bigger than this, way up by Hudson's Bay, near the Arctic Circle. The waves were twelve feet high everyday and they had to lay over till eight or nine at night. Then paddle till morning. It never gets dark there, because it's so far north. The wind died down at evening and the waves smoothed out to long swells."

This belittling of a proud achievement was taken in silence.

An older boy observed sarcastically, "Musta bin swell."

"How you know so much about it, Big Boy?" his bow partner asked. "Wuz you dare?"

"No," Jack responded lamely. "I was going to go this fall, but when my folks and I decided, there were no more places."

"Oh, too bad," another boy replied in a tone of exaggerated sympathy. There was a titter.

Dismayed at the reaction, Jack resolved to keep his mouth shut the rest of the trip and to try to be so useful that they'd forget this painful incident.

That he did so was evidenced by a couple of the Tamarack Farmers.

When he dropped off at Timberlake they shook hands with him and said they were glad he'd been along.

Back at camp, and in a continuing effort to be useful, Jack joined up with a volunteer crew who had agreed to put in a drainage ditch along the edge of a new playing field near the water front, a small field design-ed to take some of the use off the popular "Tipi Stadium," where the compaction was wearing off the turf. This was a rugged undertaking, requiring much use of pickaxes and shovels, much cutting through tree roots along the sides, much hauling in of gravel to make a bed for the orangeburg tile. Stones again around and over the tile, then gravel, loam, and sod.

The job had its good moments; for instance, that of getting to drive the old camp pickup (with the project leader sitting alongside). But it was dusty, back-breaking work. As a "crash program" it precluded any other activity in the morning, except a couple of quick swims. In the afternoons most of the gang stayed on and worked. But in a week it was *done*. It was cited in assembly as one of the most important projects of the summer. This was reward enough.

The climax of the season came for Jack when he was allowed to go off with another boy for three days and nights on a subsistence hike. Armed with much recently acquired knowledge of edible plants, equipped with a good sheath knife, fishhooks, and twine for snares, the pair set out with determined faces. The Camp knew in a general way where they would be—three similar pairs were off in other areas—so it was reasonably safe. Nevertheless it was a challenge of a kind Jack had never had before.

To make your own shelter, to keep dry and build a fire even in the rain, to find food enough to keep up strength, then to come home with a general map of the area covered—this was something. Not the least im-portant part of this adventure was really learning to be thoughtful of the other guy. After all, they were stuck with each other's company, and they might as well try to be agreeable. All four pairs returned slimmer but in fine condition, with many tales of discoveries of ingenious adaptations to circumstance. It was grist for a lodge meeting, with summaries at a sub-sequent meal to inspire the younger lodgers.

In fact, where a rugged physique and an alert mind could take one, Jack was sure to be. And his resolution to try to be useful and to try to keep his mouth shut still held. He didn't really warm up to current-events sessions. His mistake on the Assiscoos trip had made him cautious in expressing his views during general discussion. But the season, despite some deficiencies, was a success. In wildness, to paraphrase Thoreau's words, there certainly was strength for this impulsive youngster. There was also deep satisfaction, and a curbing of some of his most thoughtless action. Back next year? And how! He'd be ready for the Farm. For his money, the Farm was the most.

What appealed in this camp to which Jack had not wanted to come at all was not only the activities, but a quality, an attitude. Not being reflective, Jack couldn't put this into words—he was hardly aware of it, in fact—yet it contributed greatly to his increasing loyalty to the Camp. This was a certain subtle feeling that you were almost adult, that you should be treated as grown up until you showed you weren't ready for this trust. It was assumed that the grubby job would be done, the unscalable cliff-side surmounted. The bushwacking expedition would arrive back at camp intact and pleased with their exploit. It was expected that you would be able to plan pretty much your own activities, within a general framework which could be varied as needed. It was taken for granted that you would want to have a part in the operation of the Camp, that you would be able to discuss important issues from an adult point of view.

All in all, it was a good life. This was Jack's best summer. At the start he'd been just a kid, kind of a dumb cluck at that. Now he felt better about himself. At least he'd learned to keep his big mouth shut till he was sure he had something to say.

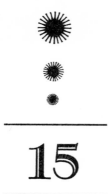

15

"On the rise of the meeting"

One cannot live very long without discovering what an appalling amount of unhappiness there is in the world. Much of it is unnecessary, but results from poor orientation in the formative years. Older people are the most common victims of this type of frustration. When a couple's children have grown up and left the nest, the parents may feel there is no longer anything to do. Nothing to do? The world around them cries out for help, but they can't hear those cries. They have not in childhood been oriented toward a sensitivity to others' needs. A child who is allowed to grow up feeling that the world revolves around him, that his needs are central and that nobody else's problems need concern him, is headed for trouble in the later years of life. His own work, he may feel, is done. He has arrived, or at least he has accomplished all for himself that he is going to be able to. There's nothing more to live for.

Children can have some of the most rewarding experiences of life if they have been encouraged to find ways in which they can give of themselves to others. This sounds "corny," as the kids would say, but it's true. It's the old Sunday-school comparison between the sweet waters of the Sea of Galilee, which has an outlet as well as an inlet, and the bitter brine of the Dead Sea, which receives but gives nothing in return.

Trying to be responsive to the needs of others may give one not only a deep satisfaction in having accomplished something worthwhile, but it may be fun in the doing.

One of the memories that boys at Saltash Mountain Camp treasure most is that of helping a local farmer with his haying. It was hot, dusty, heavy work, and not without its element of danger for a careless novice. At noon the farmer's wife, a motherly woman who had raised several sons of her own, invited the workers to a country spread which destroyed all interest in the box of sandwiches the Camp had sent along. The haying took nearly two weeks, with time out for poor weather. It gave different groups at the Camp the chance to share in an unusual experience for city youngsters. Now it is an annual event, something campers in the oldest cabins look forward to each year. Like most such projects, its benefits to both sides are numerous. It has changed the view townspeople had of the Camp from just a bunch of kids who sometimes run around "bare naked" to that of a friendly, well-behaved group who can turn out a good day's work. To city boys the insight into the difficulties of farming and the problems of rural living is invaluable. It is a gateway into a whole new world, the understanding of a type of life they had hardly known existed.

In a country community where the tradition of self-help and independence is strong, it is not always easy to find significant work projects where the help of a group of well-meaning but unskilled adolescents may be welcome. Somebody has to have his roots down in the neighboring community in order to be aware of opportunities to help. Sometimes help is needed by an individual in the village, someone secure enough in his own estimation or close enough to the camper group to be able to accept such help. One such instance was that of a local widow who by having cooked at Tamarack Farm had endeared herself to a generation of campers. When some of the girls learned of the woman's effort to get her house painted at a price she could afford, they spread the word. The matter was discussed with the director, and transportation worked out. The job was attacked with great enthusiasm if not with professional competence. Not only did these older campers paint the house, bringing over their own brushes and ladders, but they found work that needed doing inside the house. They ended by weeding the flower borders and mowing the lawn. Everyone on these trips found something he or she could do. Everyone finished with a warm feeling of satisfaction in having been useful.

This paint-up, clean-up bit led to another opportunity for community service. The basement of a church in a neighboring town had not been cleaned out for many years. It was grubby, dirty work, but "interesting." It took a crew with a truck several days to clean out the cellar, then dispose of worthless junk. It won the well-expressed gratitude of the whole congregation, an added satisfaction.

With the recent emphasis on improvement of the environment, the group at Tamarack noted that the public road which passes the camps had escaped the attention of the spring road crew charged with cleaning up the roadsides. In time for a recycling demonstration at the Fair, campers from Tamarack combed the deep grass and weeds along the roadside and came up with an incredible ten barrels of trash picked up along a five-mile stretch. Additional benefit—these youngsters will never be litter-bugs.

Vermont has a reputation for friendship with black people, a reputation which, regrettably, is not always justified. When local villagers discovered that a black girl at Indian Brook had a beautiful voice and had interested other girls in part singing, the group of singers was invited to share in an annual summer service at the local church. The girls dug out what appropriate city clothes they could find, and a good time was had by all.

People in Plymouth, and others who came to the Coolidge Centennial at the "Notch," still speak of the contribution of the Farm and Wilderness Square Dance Band, some thirty-five staff and campers who play so competently together that old-timers were fascinated. Some of the townspeople spent the afternoon listening to these young musicians re-creating the tunes of long ago. Whether the campers or the townspeople benefitted more by this service, it was one of those happy occasions where the pleasure of giving was at least as great as that of receiving.

For several summers Tamarack Farmers joined with a neighboring town to work out a program of recreation and instruction in games for area children. This led to sessions at the Camps, where these children could have instruction in swimming and in campcraft skills. Here is an area that can be developed further.

A friendly concern on the part of a year-round staff member led to a Tamarack Farm group going to Rutland to the Child Care Center during a summer when there was need of both additional help with young children and of better play facilities for the new Center. Tamarack Farmers contributed both. The Rutland *Herald* sent a reporter up to take pictures of these campers working on a playhouse they constructed during the summer. At the end of the season several of the group spent fair preparation week at the camp sawing and notching logs for a log cabin. This was put together as part of the Farm's food service concession at the Fair, then taken apart and set up as a permanent facility at the Center.

Cooperating with the Long Trail Association and with the Vermont Department of Forests and Parks has become a tradition at the Camps. Feeling that camps that use the hiking trails so extensively should do something in return, the director of one of the camps discovered that camper help if properly directed would be welcome. For some time now the Camps have been responsible for maintaining a section of the Long Trail near the Camps, and have brushed out a spur trail, the so-called Shrewsbury Cutoff. Several expeditions to Long Trail shelters which campers had noted needed cleaning up and repair led to a spectacular project in which the National Forest Service flew materials in by helicopter for a replacement shelter. The Rutland *Herald* photographers who wrote up the project as a picture story added a fringe benefit to what was already a remarkably satisfying experience.

Since the Camps use the Coolidge State Forest shelters more than any other group, it seemed right that campers should share in their maintenance also. From simple jobs like patching a few shingles into a roof and improving latrines, the Camps have graduated to a position of full trust by the State Forest authorities. One of the shelters which the CCC had built was originally quite isolated. With the advent of vehicles which can manage rough terrain, the old shelter became a good spot for beer parties and general carousing. It was agreed that camp groups would now take this dilapidated building down, then replace it with another in a less conspicuous spot not too far from the original site, but well off the road.

"You can put up the new shelter to Park specifications. Plenty of logs handy by. Cut what you need."

The confidence the Forest Service had in their skills and their judgment was not lost on these older campers. Nor was the further compliment paid them by the Service when this exciting two-year project was completed. The new assignment was that of thinning a contiguous stand of red pine. The Camps were allowed to truck out the poles they had cut in thinning the stand. Soon three rotating crews were engaged: the thinners, the truckers, and the barkers who, back at camp, peeled the poles and smoothed them for use as tipi poles or fence rails.

Many other useful contributions have been possible over the years. One that had an interesting side benefit was that of fighting a stubborn forest fire which got started in a rocky section of the Long Trail just above Sherburne Pass. For two days and nights crews from the Camps fought this fire in round-the-clock shifts. For this service of love they were paid handsomely by the State, much to their surprise. The campers involved voted to turn the money over to the Camps' scholarship fund.

But another and rather unusual local service has gone on now for a number of years. Many summers ago Mickey Cochrane, at that time associate director of Timberlake, became interested in a set of ancient cellar holes in the Five Corners area of the State Forest, an area heavily wooded, where a rushing stream made an attractive objective for a hike. About a mile away from these cellar holes and the stream that ran past them, Mickey and a group of hikers discovered an old burying ground. It was located in what had been a sightly sweep of meadow, but the farmer who owned it couldn't mow among the gravestones, so the little plot had been neglected. At the time Mickey came on it, the stones were half hidden by brush and by larger trees which in some cases had tilted or even overturned the stones. Every year a group of Timberlake boys have hacked away at the trees and brush, reclaiming each season a further portion from the wilderness.

The little cemetery turned out to have an interesting history. Rubbings which the boys had made of some of the slabs revealed dates almost obliterated in the soft stone. Whole families, apparently, had died within a few weeks of each other. An epidemic? It had evidently wiped out the whole community, leaving nobody to care about those stones with their mute witness to tragedy. A stroke of good fortune brought the answer. In Ludlow on a day off Mickey was directed to the home of an old lady who knew Five Corners. She showed him a photograph of the houses which had once covered the cellar holes. She even knew the names of the families who had owned them. They were all familiar names; they were those on the gravestones. Yes, it had been an epidemic, diphtheria, against which there was at that time no defense in an isolated logging village. The boys studied their rubbings with new interest, and with perhaps the first reflections on the fleeting quality of life, the meaning of death. Gray's

"Elegy Written in a Country Churchyard" was suddenly significant, even strangely stirring.

A favorite Quaker story is that of the stranger who wandered into a Friends Meeting for Worship. The newcomer became restless as the silence wore on. Nothing was happening, nobody did anything. Finally he leaned over to whisper to his neighbor: When does the service start?

"Immediately on the rise of the Meeting," the old Friend replied and lapsed back into silence.

The story seems appropriate, and quite literally applicable when Tamarack Farm has been holding an early morning Meeting for Worship in the sightly area above the lake. The meeting ends with silent handshakes. Campers stream up the steps by the maintenance building to pick up the stock of tools lying along the tool-house porch in neat piles beneath the names of the various crews of the day. While some crews shoulder their shovels or their scythes and brush hooks and stride off on foot, another crew may pile into a waiting truck to be taken to some "off-campus" service location.

As these youngsters settle in for the ride, the look of anticipation on their faces signifies that they have discovered the meaning of that crazy saying of the old folks: It's more blessed to give than to receive.

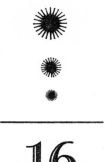

16

Flexibility

My own introduction to organized camping came during college. Perhaps my longing for a summer outdoors was a reaction to academic confinement. At any rate when spring came, the lure of the out of doors combined with a liking for youngsters to make a job as "nature" counselor in a small private camp look good. Thinking back on that job interview from the vantage point of forty years of experience as a camp director I might not have hired me. No camp experience, no leadership experience, a very unorganized knowledge of the bees, the birds, and the bugs, and an inexhaustible naivete.

But the camp wasn't all that good either. About the sixth week of the eight-week season, time began to drag. Boredom set in. The boys were counting the days to the end of camp. Old timers on the staff explained: "This is the 'sixth-week sag.'"

That the season was flat, stale, and unprofitable was only partly my fault. There was a dearth of imagination in planning the days, the weeks, the season. The rigid, repetitive schedule allowed no flexibility. As I thought over the experience later on, I decided that camping itself was *great*. The trouble was that the season had lacked variety. There were no changes of pace, no surprises to break the routine. Someday, I decided,

I'd set up a camp with such constant change and development in the program that nobody would have time to get tired of it. Whatever the faults of Timberlake, the first of the Farm and Wilderness Camps, dullness isn't one of them.

Each week is a unit by itself, with its own goals and achievement. The first week emphasizes activities by cabin groups. Staff and campers in each cabin are getting acquainted. Even old boys find new combinations of talent and possibilities in the cabin. Time is spent checking the surroundings to see how they can be changed or improved, working whenever the gang can be together. A better fireplace perhaps, new short logs for the cabin council ring. A cleanup of all dead wood within easy distance, with crews to break it up and stack it neatly under the cabin. What else can we do as a cabin improvement? Perhaps lash a new washstand, with cubbyholes for soap protected from the rain, a backboard with overhang to keep towels from wind and storm.

A cabin tour of the surroundings is planned for that first morning. The TL farm, the gardens, the cove, the rope course and the outdoor gym; the campcraft area with its varied fireplaces. The nature trail is admired.

There may be short trips that first week, perhaps an overnight at one of the Lake shelters, or, depending on the age and experience of the cabin group, a night at a more distant shelter with an early breakfast to get back in time for Meeting for Worship.

During this time the boys are also getting used to the all-camp and the lodge activities. There will be large groups in the morning for projects or campcraft, gardens or water front and sports or natural science. Then in the afternoon a variety of perhaps a dozen small-group activities by individual choice, with brief descriptions of each in the dining hall at the end of lunch.

The second week will be sure to offer an overnight trip for the Big and Senior lodges. The First Lodge, according to staff judgment of readiness, may enjoy a first overnight at one of the lake shelters.

In the third week most of the groups will be off for "sign-up" trips of two or three nights, depending again on skill and experience. The first fleets of canoes are off on distant waterways. These early trips are largely for old-timers, but it is necessary to get them started promptly so experienced half-seasoners may get a chance for a canoe trip. Before the end of the season every camper who has passed the strict requirements in swimming, canoeing, and campcraft will have a week's canoeing.

The fourth week is change-over week, ending the first half-season. Canoe trips continue, of course, during this week: once the fleets are out, they must be kept in use. But everyone else is in camp. It is a time for finishing major work projects, for mastering new skills, for enjoying the water front, the outdoor gym, the rope and the obstacle courses, and games. Sign ups are posted for the big trips of the next two weeks, and campers are busy planning, getting gear in shape, studying maps and waterways.

During the next two weeks in-camp activities are pretty much catch-as-catch-can. Trips are going out constantly, others returning, the most trip-minded individuals "laying over" for a day, then setting out on some new and different exploration. Those in camp will enjoy the delight of having a water front or a games area for just a small group; but the talk will concern the state of particular trails, the mess a canoe trip found (and cleaned up) at some beloved camping site, the latest bushwhacking expedition home from Ascutney or down Money Brook in the Nineveh wilderness.

The seventh week all are back except a few who come in during the week from a late canoe trip. It is Fair week. Starting from scratch on Monday morning, the Fair grows and grows during the week with everybody working on some part of it. In the afternoons various cabin groups may be back to push things along. Other may enjoy late season sports; harvesting expeditions will visit the gardens. Some group may sort over the broilers for a cabin cookout or a "garden party." This last will mean supper from the garden, cooked in the pasture above the TL gardens. The last square dances will be taking place this week. The older campers will work out picnics and an evening with opposite numbers at Indian Brook. The excitement of this week peaks at the Fair on Saturday. It is the climax of the whole season's activity.

The final week starts with everybody collapsing for most of Sunday, although that afternoon there may be various local expeditions to favorite spots. Monday morning is Fair cleanup; by noon nearly everything is back in place. During the week there will be a deal of activity to finish campcraft or water-front tests delayed by trips, to complete a bridge or work on a path abandoned for hikes. Or one can enjoy for the last time some cherished sport—archery, or soccer, or a final game of softball. The evenings of this week are pretty well settled by custom. One will be Spy Night, one a big powwow on the season's successes and deficiencies. Then the banquets. And the next day, going home. It's a full season, full but not crowded. Excitement has risen until the day of the Fair. Then it tapers off in a deliberate letdown. Everybody gets unwound again so he can go home rested, not worn out, bubbling with stories to tell of high moments during the season.

Within each week also there is variety. Sunday is a day of relaxation. Cabin cleanup is extended to include getting out the laundry, tidying up the area around the cabin, perhaps scrubbing down the floor with soap and warm water, and just enjoying each other's company or discussing plans for the coming week. The afternoon is free generally for short trips up the Ridge or to Mad Morgan's Potato Patch or the Caves, or fooling around the water front and soaking up some tan. Or perhaps there will be an all-camp activity, like a good water meet if the weather's fine, or "junior Olympics" or a track meet on the soccer field, or a late afternoon barbecue with preparations which involve pretty much everybody in one lodge, either in food-getting from the gardens or rustling wood for the fire pits. If the afternoon is "structured," with some kind of athletic event for instance, then the evening is free. If the afternoon was free, the evening may see some sort of talent show or a long story for the whole crowd, or perhaps music from those who have instruments at camp. Or there may be a chance to learn new songs and sing again the old favorites.

Each weekday morning the big group activities mentioned before will keep everybody busy. The afternoons are free for small-group or individual activities, some available only once or twice a week. The evenings are varied too. Mondays, current events, with a not-too-exciting alternative for those who aren't interested in overhauling the news. Tuesday evenings are generally free. Many groups will be cooking out or going off on overnight hikes. Wednesday night is also unscheduled. Thursdays some other type of meeting with the Big Lodge at Indian Brook, may take place, or on alternate Thursdays, a square dance. The Senior Lodge will be having a lodge evening, a good game followed by a discussion and lodge meeting, or, if the weather is poor, a whole evening together, working out group problems, then following up with a bull session. Friday evenings, the plan is reversed, with the Senior Lodge having its weekly square dance. Saturday afternoons are set aside for the all-camp game, a different one each week.

Saturday evening there is a council fire at which, after some music by the guitarists and banjo players, and probably a song or two, the all-camp powwow follows up the Cabin Representatives meeting that took place during rest hour. This may lead to discussion of items of camp planning, but there is always time for a talent show with a story to top it off.

Cutting across all this in the early weeks may be several "cabin days" when the whole camp heads off by cabin groups, or elects to take advantage of a nearly deserted water front or games field to work out an in-camp program just for the cabin. Such occasions may be repeated once or even twice during the last four weeks, though the need is not so great in this part of the season.

Further accenting the weeks, a number of special occasions stand out. First, of course, Independence Day. It comes too early to be much more than an interruption. It does have the benefit, however, of getting the three Plymouth camps together so they can begin to know one another and to realize that they are part of a family of camps. After a "regular" day at each camp until after afternoon swim, the groups head down to the Fair grounds with sweaters, flashlights, and anticipation. They are quickly drawn into various loosely organized large-group games. Supper, served from the area of the barbecue pits, is followed by more games, or by singing together, a dramatic skit or two, and a talk on the meaning of independence. As darkness gathers, a big bonfire is touched off. Flames leap high into the evening sky. Showers of sparks threaten to fall on the spellbound watchers below, yet somehow, nobody is touched. While the attention of all is focused on the fire, suddenly with a swish and a roar the first of the sky rockets goes off, followed by a boom that reechoes across the valley. For the next half hour the sky is aglitter with the display. When the last reverberations have died away down the valley, and the night is suddenly silent again, flashlights come out, cabin counselors call to their groups, and the trek back to camp begins.

The midseason festival on the third Saturday of camp has often taken the form of an old country sports day. This form started when an English counselor from the Midlands described such an occasion in rural England. Preceded by a parade down the camp road, and highlighted by pea-shucking contests, cross-country runs that include a swim from the end of Bear Pit Point to Paradise Island, the occasion features a supper eaten in little knots and clusters over the whole area. Then there is some sort of presentation by each camp in the evening. Memory of this is long cherished by first half-seasoners, who will be leaving during the following week.

The Fair deserves a chapter by itself. Planned soon after the start of the second half, worked on intensively all of Fair week, this grand occasion can scarcely be rivaled anywhere for color, variety, ingenuity, and action. Over the more than thirty years of its operation, some half-dozen permanent structures have been put up by camper groups inspired with an idea. The flying machine, the hay flier, the dizzy machine, the dunkum, the strength tester, the aqua-chute, and the ferris wheel are old favorites. Each year there is the keenest rivalry among the Big and Senior Lodge cabins for their operation.

The circumstances of their building often provide some striking illustration of youthful determination or of a counselor's idea so good that it just has to be worked out. A prime example is the ferris wheel, which isn't a wheel at all, but a heavy wooden square perpendicular to the ground, its abutments solidly secured in cement, its axle a heavy iron bar, its mode of turning, boy power! This contraption, though striking in concept, seemed so difficult for a set of eleven-year-olds to build, so liable to hidden dangers, that when Tom Carrow, the Foxes' counselor, outlined his plans to the director of Timberlake a fortnight before the Fair, that worthy, though publicly pledged to consider even "screwy" ideas, tried to brush off the whole matter by sending Tom to the Camp's "engineer in residence," a capable older man who teaches engineering in a large university. To the director's surprise, the engineer after a thorough study of Tom's diagrams, pronounced them "safe if erected in accordance with agreed plans."

"Tom, if you do this, it is going to mean no final trip for the Foxes. They'll have to spend all their time, all day long every day, on getting that thing up. It's a great idea, but do count the cost; be sure the Foxes understand the cost and are willing to pay it."

Tom returned that evening after a cabin meeting with a new gleam in his eye. "They want to do it, and we'll spend the time. John's going to get the materials tomorrow morning and we'll start work on the excavation. Three Foxes are giving up a canoe trip, but they're willing. They really are."

"You're sure you didn't twist their arms?"

"No, not really. I just sold 'em an idea." Tom grinned, "They're all jumping up and down with excitement. This is going to be the most spectacular thing in the Fair. It will rise thirty feet from the ground. All we need is an assist from the Farm to snap it into place."

The power of a Great Idea was demonstrated during that fortnight. The Foxes were out on the Fair grounds all day every day of the week preceding Fair Week. Boys going out or returning from trips looked over curiously at the cluster of eleven- and twelve-year-olds swarming over a hillock above the agricultural exhibits. When the whole camp arrived bright-eyed and bushy-tailed the Monday morning of the Great Week, the foundations for this structure were already set. The huge "wheel" was laid out on the ground, being bolted together. The four chairs were being assembled. To the many queries of "Whatcha doin'?" the response was a laconic "Ferris wheel," really more mystifying than before.

Would they make it? Would the thing be declared "safe" when up? And would it work? These were the great questions which overshadowed nearly every other preparation that year. A day of rain put them behind. When the second rainy day began, the boys decided they had to work through it. Raincoats and rain hats, or natural raincoats, which never leak, served through all but the heaviest gusts of windblown rain. These drove the workers to the doorway of the barn facing the Fair grounds, there to stand in disconsolate frustration until the hardest downpour was over.

Came the morning of the Fair, bright and sunny. The gleaming "wheel" was in place, towering over surrounding construction. But the four chairs had much work still to do to enable them to "hang loose" and still be safe. The Fair opened, and still the Foxes were working feverishly on the chairs. Not even a glance toward the exciting brouhaha of the clowns at the opening ceremonies.

A half hour after the Fair had opened, the new structure was pronounced safe and ready for customers. The criers with their megaphones and stentorian voices threaded through the Fair crowds to announce the gala opening. Everyone turned to view the great structure, beribboned with many-colored streamers. The lines formed. They could have charged a dollar a customer that day and paid off the whole expense in the one afternoon with money left over for the camp's scholarship fund. But the money was incidental. The Foxes had proved what group determination and the discipline of a Great Idea could do for a cabin of boys. They had done the un-do-able, performed the impossible.

"The difficult we do right away; the impossible takes half an hour longer," they misquoted, rejoicing.

Displays of livestock, garden produce, art, photography, Indian crafts and natural science serve to summarize part of the season's activities, as do the demonstrations in campcraft, projects, Indian dances, and folk dancing. The Fair serves to bring the six camps together and to point out once more the fact of belonging to one family with similar ideals, values, and traditions. Perhaps the most persistent tradition is that of flexibility.

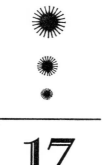

17

Leadership

Readers may have noted how frequently in the foregoing pages leadership has been mentioned as the key to achieving some goal for a youngster or a group. Are all counselors so able, mature, dedicated, competent that they can get the most out of each situation, every teachable moment? Obvious rhetorical question! But when a new counselor turns out to have some of the above qualities, counseling with him by the director or one of the older staff pays big dividends. Such a person is likely to stay on for as many years as professional plans permit. The continuing association, often strengthened during the year through correspondence, delights both sides.

"You know you can practically write your own ticket. We want you back," the director is likely to say at the end of each season.

Such a staff member, gifted with the insight a genuine love of youngsters can give, equipped with outdoor skills, evidencing high ideals, maturity, devotion, above all forgetfulness of self and joy in seeing some difficult youngster "straighten out" during a summer — this paragon is not too common.

How does a camp find such staff? Most often through some well-seasoned staff member whose judgment can be relied on. Less frequently from a college placement office or a camping agency. These applications require very careful screening. Even references and an interview will not always point up the flaws with which the camp cannot live, though one becomes more expert at asking the right questions and interpreting responses. Also, there are warning questions from the applicant. How far is it to the nearest town? Is it a big town? Does the Camp provide transportation? What is the time off? Are the evenings free?

References need a lot of interpretation too, and a deal of reading between the lines. Nobody wants to blackball a young applicant, who may, in fact, have learned something by previous job difficulties. Cutting through many of the time-wasting questions to which a respondent can phrase a careful answer, one question includes all the rest. "If you had a son or a daughter, would you be willing to have this youngster pattern after the applicant?"

Undoubtedly the best source of new staff is the camp's own CIT or CA group. The Counselor Apprentices, all seventeen or entering the twelfth grade, have usually survived the Counselor in Training course at Tamarack Farm the year before. Probably they have several years of previous experience at one or more of the Farm and Wilderness Camps. We know their strengths; their weaknesses we have decided we can work with. The ten boys at Timberlake and the ten girls at Indian Brook (and the occasional smaller group at one or more of the other Camps) are in charge of some able, seasoned, understanding counselor devoted to the ideals of the Camps and steeped in their tradition.

The bond between this leader and his or her charges is a close one, so close, in fact, that some of the dedication of the leader rubs off on the pupils. There is also something of the spirit of the Outward Bound groups here: the ability to take the rigors of wilderness training, to survive through one's own resources, to meet any emergency the wilds can produce, all with calm efficiency, with trained skills, with cheerful optimism in the face of real danger.

It has been said with only a reasonable degree of exaggeration that you could drop any one of the Apprentices in the wilds with a minimum of equipment or none at all, and he would present himself back at camp within a very short time and in good condition, healthy, happy, and able to give a modest account of the reasoning, the ingenuities, and the skills by which he found his way back. But space lacks for a full outline of the varied summer a Counselor Apprentice will have. Suffice it to say here that the CAs are generally the finest counselors the Camps have. Out of the ten there will be only one or two who will be counseled out during the season, sent home at the end of the season with the satisfaction of having grown during the summer, though perhaps not quite enough to be ready for a junior counselorship the next year. Or perhaps the CA goes home with a better realization of some other talent he may have, not in the area of leadership.

The staff is, of course, the determining factor in summer camps between opportunities lost or a learning experience so rich for a boy or a girl that its possibilities and its blessings can never be fully recorded. Built up over years of trial and error, seasoned, worked with, and cherished, the staff in the last analysis always leaves one filled with awe. How do such wonderful people happen? And what has a director done to deserve such colleagues?

A staff is far more than the sum of its many parts, its individual counselors. It has a personality which is a blending of many types, shrewdly selected, or picked by chance and then appreciated. Here is the rough-and-ready, happy-go-lucky Pied Piper of Hamlin who can get a guy to do any grubby job and love it. There is the sensitive, quiet sort of man, or woman, whose appeal is to the thoughtful, reflective youngster. Occasionally there is the clown and the show-off, the mimic, who can keep a whole dining hall rocking with laughter. And there is the music lover, who can play a number of instruments, who can talk knowledgeably with a certain minority in the camp. He speaks their language. They have a secret bond. They live in a world from which others are barred not by design, but by lack of some deep impulse the in-group shares.

Now and then in traveling about a camp one comes on a counselor sitting quietly with a camper in some nook a bit apart from the crowd. Almost always the grownup is listening. Occasionally he raises his head for a quick glance into the other's eyes, or nods understandingly. Something in the adult's approach has loosened the child's tongue. Deep impulses, carefully hidden from the world, pour out. The counselor asks a question designed to start further reflection. The boy, or girl, finding a way through some maze, is guided occasionally by a simple comment or some shrewd question. When the meeting is over, the camper may walk off thoughtfully, or perhaps disappear into the woods and spend an hour putting together new pieces of the puzzle, parts not clearly seen before.

The counselor has sensed the teachable moment. His other work, some activity he is scheduled for, can get on without him. His colleagues will understand.

Frequently the teachable moment comes at bedtime, perhaps when everyone is comfortably ensconced in blankets or sleeping bags and the person in charge asks a question about an event of the day gone by. This starts a reaction. A penetrating if informal assessment of some happening or how it went wrong, or what it did to people involved, may ensue. Comments come from the bunks, some with heat, some slowly, as new significance starts to appear. Half the cabin may be asleep before the counselor sums things up to a final comment, or a quotation from Meeting.

The special activity for which a staff member is responsible offers endless chance for driving home some truth. This cannot be a preachment, a moral, but something beyond that; a tiny glimpse of some part of the ultimate truth of which life is made, something which a bit of behavior can illustrate. All this can sound so idealistic as to be unreal. The counselor has offered nothing world-shaking or saintly, but just a quick comment which starts young minds thinking, a bit of wisdom garnered from experience and gladly shared.

While on the subject of the adults and their influence on campers, it is proper to take a look at the director, who is responsible probably for the choice of staff, the corporate personality, and the ease and efficiency with which it functions. What is a director? Is he the functionary who sits off there in the office, toting up long columns of figures, studying statements of purchases and filing them for entry into ponderous account books? Is he the man or woman who spends his day dictating letters, or writing them himself, interviewing tradesmen, phoning business houses regarding the latest discounts? We hope not. This depends somewhat on how the director views his job. Is he engaged in a business, a part of the camping "industry," as non-camping people sometimes mistakenly call the camping movement?

A director's proper role can be defined negatively. It is never to do anything which somebody else can do as well or better. He should not be a businessman, except incidentally, and in a supervisory way. This sort of talent he can hire. He should not be a bookkeeper. Except for a brief look-in every day, he should not be an office manager either.

He should be the sort of person of whom people complain bitterly that they never can find him. Of course not. The people who have first claim on him, the staff, the campers, can find him. He's out among them, watching a game, stopping to see how a particular camper is doing in archery, storing up some impressions for a talk with the head of an activity later on, dropping a comment which relates some action to the goals of the camp, sitting down beside the youngster moping on the edge of the playing field, taking part for a time in some work job, or catching a frisbee a few times and twisting it back. He is where the action is.

At rest hour or bedtime, he may drop in on a cabin for a moment or two of chatting with the leader and his charges. His role is supervisory, inspirational, interpretative. He knows what is going on, sees some of the play of interpersonal relations. He counsels the counselors, listening to them, offering bits of advice or asking questions; he chats with a staff member in a relaxed manner which has no motive beyond getting to know and enjoy a fine person. Yet the way he cites an ideal of the camp, using it to illuminate some item of policy, may inspire a young staff member, or some camper he has been talking with.

Gradually, at the start of a new season, the director with the help of veteran members of the staff, manages to convince newcomers of the significance of what they are doing, spotlighting for them the nature and the extent of the responsibility they have assumed for young lives. This happens particularly at a staff meeting, where the agenda has been stripped of all possible administrivia and the time is spent on assessing the impact of various parts of program, truing up this part, focusing on that; considering individual campers, sometimes in depth, with a view to bringing the resources of the staff and the camp to bear on an emerging problem.

Yet somehow, the occasion is not all deadly serious. If the director can keep himself reasonably rested, and the importance of so doing is revealed at these times, he can rise to the bait of humor and banter. The whole staff sees the funny side of a situation. They relax frequently in laughter, so that at times, to somebody standing outside the building where the meeting is going on, it must seem as if the august group inside is doing nothing but telling funny stories. Laughter is in itself relaxing. Everyone is put at ease. More, much more, is achieved than if everything were deadly serious. This is a consummation devoutly to be wished. It is not always reached, but it should be the director's goal above all else.

In all-camp assemblies the director's role of interpreter is particularly important. The ideals of the camp he approaches in half a hundred ways at different times and on varying occasions. The goals, the objectives, the values giving life and meaning to policies, he contrives to hold before the group. Never laboring his points, often seeming not to focus on them at all, he manages, nevertheless, to keep them as a touchstone for all that goes on. They buttress his thinking; they underlie assumptions which are skirted perhaps, not stated, but always there, and influential enough so that his listeners become aware of them.

The camp is, then, in a very real sense, the director. His love of children inspires every decision. His understanding of them guides his actions. His interpretation of the fundamental ideals of the institution inspires staff and eventually campers. His fairness and honesty create an environment in which fine people can work happily, and whose happiness is reflected in the relaxed, smiling faces of campers. He provides for campers and staff alike, a seed bed where great ideals can grow and expand. And he is the only one who can do this with full effect. Far from seeing his role limited by the constant application of the negative definition cited earlier, never to do what somebody else can do as well or better, far from finding himself with little to do, his role assumes proportions which make it always just beyond reach, a sobering responsibility to try to grow into.

Nobody can be perfect. One can lack many of the varied talents and professional disciplines, but with this basic qualification of honest respect for the personality of a child, he can grow into most of what he needs.

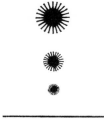

18

The camps as protest

The last day of camp is a time of upheaval. Sometimes it brings the moment of truth, confrontation with sins of omission through the season. For Jack Fox this was true. For almost the first time, Gordon Brown lost his patience with the boy. Packing for the return home was a sad duty left by custom until the last morning of camp. Then the whole gang turned to and did the job, while some junior counselor brought around baggage tags and "wrote up the baggage." There was more activity per square yard that morning in the Lumberjacks' cabin than during the whole season.

Gordie Brown was making the rounds. Kids of fourteen generally didn't need help with the actual packing, but you never know.

"For gosh sake, Jack, what's happened to all your gear?"

"What gear?" Jack inquired, straightening up to regard his counselor with innocent blue eyes.

"What gear? The stuff you brought. Your trunk didn't come up here only half full, did it?"

"His trunk was overflowing when he came," Tim Jeffers offered helpfully. "Remember we kidded him about it?"

Jack gave his comrade a quick look, the kind that says, "I'll see you outside later on."

"Well, do something about it then," Gordie pursued. "Run up and check the Lumberjacks' Lost and Found box. Look through the general Lost and Found. Gotta be some of your junk in one of them."

"I've checked both places," Jack retorted, turning sullen. "Nothing of mine in either."

"You used to have more Lost and Found than anyone else," Gordie persisted. "I thought you'd wised up this half."

"He did," Frankie Ray offered. "He lost it more thoroughly. Now nobody can find it."

There was a general laugh.

"Where are your shoes?" Gordie was relentless. "They'd help fill up some of that space. How many pairs did you bring?"

"Oh, I guess two besides the moccasins."

"Well? You can't have lost them all. Where are your moccasins?"

"Here's one I found under the cabin." With a sheepish grin Jack held up a mouldy specimen.

"You can't go home with one moccasin," Gordie went on in a tone of exasperation. "Can't you remember where you left your shoes?"

"I haven't worn any since early season when I decided to go barefoot," Jack replied lamely.

"Where were you when you decided?" Jimmy Winters asked. "If you were up the Ridge, then that's where you left them."

There was another laugh.

"We all love you, Jack, old bean," Gordie grinned, patting the boy on the bronzed shoulders. "But I'm deadly serious about this: if you guys don't take home a reasonable facsimile of what you brought, I'll be getting distressed phone calls all next week when I should be recuperating from having you fellows on my hands. And then letters from you little darlings," Gordie went on, warming up to his theme. "They'll all go something like this. 'Dear Gordie,' they'll start off, Camp was *great*. And as a counselor you're the most. I had the best summer yet. Thanks for everything. By the way, Gordie, could you send me my camera? It's under the upper corner of the mattress. And my sneakers. I think I left them on the rack under the cabin. They must have fallen down. Could you look up my green sweater? It should be tucked in behind the rafter just beyond our table. Get lots of rest, Gordie. Be seein' yuh.' My answer to that kind of garbage is a little two-letter word. So get your gear *now.* Anything found later goes off to the Friends Service Committee for other little boys and girls who will appreciate it more. This isn't only addressed to Jack. It means you, and you and everyone of you."

Jack waited patiently for Gordie to finish. The counselor was pleased enough with himself now, Jack figured, to listen to an earnest plea.

"Look, Gordie," he ventured. "I just can't find the rest of this stuff. I've looked. Honest I have. But I've got everything I *need* right here now, everything I've used in the last half of camp. Except for the sleeping bag, it can fit into my knapsack. Then I can take it all on the bus."

Evidently the wrong thing to say. Gordie turned on his charge with mock ferocity. "Look, young fellah. You better wise up to the facts of life. What you bring to camp isn't what you *need.* It's what the home folks *think* you need, unless you're bright enough to do your own packing and keep 'em out while you're doing it."

Tim Jeffers, who had made the initial remark about the overflowing trunk, was feeling guilty about the way a good pal of his was being picked on.

"Look, Jack," he volunteered. "I found a couple of my things in the Otter Lost and Found. Let's make the rounds of the other boxes. And sometimes things get down behind the piano in the Lower Lodge. O.K., Gordie? We'll be right back."

Too bad Jack's self-esteem, built up so gradually through the whole season, was thus endangered. Beaten down at school, and to some extent at home by demands that seemed to him irrelevant, Jack had here at camp for the first time found an environment in which there were things he could do well. There were values he could appreciate. Once he sensed these different values, he forgot his earlier scorn for the place and settled in with happy acceptance. Stages in this conversion could be traced by the boy's own action. The witch-grass row in the garden was the first evidence. This, however, was done to gain the approval of his cabin counselor. The change was complete when Jack came up from the water front and joined in a game of frisbee in the Tipi Stadium without bothering to put on a pair of pants. His devotion to the ideals of the Camp was signalized by his adoption of a pair of shorts as full dress, with a sweat shirt added for cool mornings. The boy's change in attitude was evidenced also by the alacrity with which he responded when there was some grubby job to be done, like helping dig the drainage ditch for the new playing field.

If one regards the underlying ideals of the Farm and Wilderness Camps as protest against things as they are, protest which has evoked a creative response to demonstrate the feasibility of things as they might be, then Jack Fox is the perfect example of a youngster whose potential is lost in the ordinary formal school, but brought out to its fullest in an educational setup which puts the horse before the cart instead of vice versa.

The usual old-style school, of which, happily, there are fewer examples now, crammed knowledge down the unwilling gullets of children who had no desire for it. This lack of desire was known as the "resistance to learning." It was supposed to be one of the occupational drawbacks teachers had to bear. And education was regarded as a body of knowledge, most of it inherited, some regarded as useful to the nation, and the nation's business. But it was seldom functional. Its clientele had no sense of its being useful to the recipient. Nor did anybody ask whether this body of knowledge was really "education."

It is the assumptions behind education against which the Camps have protested. First of all, we challenge the assumption that education for everybody is a body of middle-class knowledge which all must absorb in order to be successful. It is probable that a fairly small portion of the spectrum can succeed at this, while all the rest gain only the sense of failure. In place of this view of education, the Camps have set the belief that the first duty of educators is to give children a feeling of success, of competence in some field their abilities open to them. Once this precious self-esteem is established, they can begin on the other aspect of education, that of making decisions by weighing all factors—the demands of the situation, the involvement of basic values, the effect on others whose rights and feelings must be considered. Education, then, becomes a process of increasingly effective decision making, and the place to get it is where life goes on all about us, not, certainly, in the sterile, artificial atmosphere of a room with rows of desks where kids can be isolated from each other, and the interplay of personal relations is reduced to a minimum.

Corollary to this view is the conviction that the best educational environment is one which permits of the widest scope of decision-making within a child's or a group's area of competence. And after a few mistakes, this area of competence grows rapidly.

Having set up artificial and utterly wrong goals, the school is forced to use any means to get its victims to achieve these purposes. The two tools that come easiest to hand are those of personal effort in scholarship, — "marks" — and competition. At the Camps competitive sports are of small moment. Instead, campers discover what miracles can be wrought by cooperation. Cooperation leads to a surprising spirit of friendliness and sensitivity to the needs and aspirations of others.

Besides protesting the continuing crimes of formal education, the Camps have always tried to set up a counter to the softness and over-protection which, particularly in this age of deteriorating cities, seems a necessary part of urban living. This is the ideal of ruggedness, of physical challenge, of being able to "take it," goals which have become proud traditions.

In fact, the Camps have protested all that is artificial in urban living, particularly life cluttered with unneeded things and crowded calendars. It is good to return to the ideal of Quaker simplicity, to see what human ingenuity can do to effect reasonable comfort and safety in the wilderness, what the establishment of priorities can bring about in enabling one to get along without much of the clothing, gadgetry, and endless pills and nostrums with which Madison Avenue has burdened us.

The pretense and hypocrisy which the new generation is protesting is countered at the Camps by as complete honesty of interpersonal relations as tact and sensitivity to others' feelings permit.

The lack of motivation, the drifting, which are also a product in part of the educational system, are swallowed up at Camp in the joy of cooperative effort. The satisfactions of work well done catch on. Alienation melts away before the genuine enthusiasm for involvement, involvement in improving some aspect of the environment with a determination which doesn't count the cost. During a season an older camper may begin to sense some purpose in life, may even generate a type of Quaker social concern, sensitive, understanding, creative.

Prejudices regarding race, color, nationality and creed tend to disappear in an atmosphere of acceptance, where one can become pals with fine representatives of other cultures and thus gain a respect for other points of view.

Injustice, another concern of the present generation, stands out more clearly as an abomination not to be tolerated when the organization of the Camps is truly democratic. Certainly the future of our nation is safer in the hands of an electorate sensitive to the needs and aspirations of other groups than in the hands of a generation who have been forced to repeat a pledge of allegiance and to salute a flag with no reference to whether these symbols are still entirely worthy of such respect.

Long before the present concern about pollution and the destruction of the environment, the Camps were stressing the study of natural science as a way of instilling in youngsters an appreciation of and respect for the natural environment. You destroy what you don't understand and therefore don't respect. At the Camps children make a wide detour around a nesting bird, or a patch of maidenhair ferns. In camping they learn to restore a campsite to the condition in which they found it so the next comers will scarcely be aware that somebody has camped there before.

It was, in fact, this general callousness toward the environment, toward people of different skin color or different economic status, toward other groups who should be part of a democratic society, which has led to an emphasis on the idea of reverence. Respect for all life ripens quickly into reverence when one begins to understand the implications.

The attitude of reverence for all life becomes particularized in a reverence for human personality, for the contributions of different types of people, different races, creeds, and for the myriad forms of animal and plant life. This includes reverence also for the mysterious power that undergirds life itself.

All this attitude of reverence and wonder which so enriches life and fulfills the human potential is vitiated by the prevalence of the philosophy of materialism, easy to accept in an era of middle-class affluence. The Camps have always protested this philosophy, which is so limiting in its view of life, so wanting in any help in time of stress. While not promoting any specific creed, or in fact, any set of "answers," the little daily Meeting for Worship for many is a time of sincere search for meanings which lie beneath the surface, for truths that don't change with the season or the generation, but which gradually spread in significance until they illumine all of life.

It must be the set of values detailed above that has led people to speak of the Camps as "a way of life." Certainly it is these values, so evident to the present generation, which account for the continuance of the Camps in a time when many such organizations are not finding this a period of expansion.

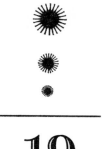

19

End of camp

"Invested with magical powers or properties," as the *Oxford Diction-ary* puts it, certainly describes the effect of a camp season on most youngsters. The changes can be so many and so far-reaching as to seem almost like sorcery. It isn't just the summer tan and the clear eye and the general bloom of health. It's not only the springy step, the better coordination, the way a youngster stands. Nor is it just the new skills he has acquired, the competence in the water, the way he has learned to handle a canoe, his ability to take care of himself in the wilderness. The real changes are not for one to see. They come out later, their subtle presence attested by a difference in attitudes, in the way a boy or girl may regard a parent or a job at home or what the gang is doing. The camper has accepted a set of values, probably unconsciously, but whole-heartedly. They can change a life.

Sometimes the surprise lies in what a camp does for a boy or girl with whom its chance of success may have seemed not too good when he came. The very shy boy or girl, timid, defeated, withdrawn, has become not outgoing and boisterous but imbued with a quiet confidence which enables him to hold his own in a gathering.

The urban sophisticate, scorning simple, wholesome activities as "kid stuff," has been won over. After the first week or so he becomes an enthusiastic participant. He has responded to the honesty of some fine counselor. With this response his whole superficial system of values has fallen, and he has accepted another system in its place.

The young person with a single interest, the near genius in math or art or science, has learned to enjoy other aspects of life. And the devil-may-care, reckless, impulsive boy has learned to stop a moment and reflect before acting.

Certainly Jack Fox of the early square dance is a good example of this last type. Before the end of the second week his supercilious air had gone. Because he admired adults on the staff who subscribe to the mores and the ideals of the camp, he has accepted these ideals too, along with the persons who have them. The instinct of imitation is strong. The element of hero worship moves undiminished in the early teens.

The end-of-season banquet reviews the summer, recalls gay adventures together, underlines camp ideals, honoring those persons who have best exemplified them. One means is through the awards. These are mostly group awards—axes to a half-dozen boys who have won the highest rating in campcraft; little retracting reel tape measures to campers of outstanding achievement in projects; the Red Cross cards to persevering swimmers. For everyone there is an achievement plaque listing activities in which each camper has shown more than a passing interest.

There are moments of hilarity too, mock awards that single out some characteristic of a group. At the long tables with their rustic decorations and their campers scrubbed and brushed, there is eager anticipation as lists are read out of boys who are to step forward and receive some token appropriate to their habits. Tiny pillows signalize the "sack hounds." "Chow hounds" receive plastic forks. Miniature shovels go to those inclined to add to the truth. Green thumbs knitted at the sister camp mark the ardent gardeners.

For members of the "Lonely Hearts Club," those who have had special interests at the sister camp on the far shore of the lake, there are red paper hearts cut in half. The second half is being given out to the girl friend at the other end of the lake.

Jack's own heart pounded with embarrassment as he heard his name called for the award of half a heart. His cabin mates clapped and cheered as he returned from receiving the emblem, a self-conscious but pleased smirk on his face.

While the gang turned quickly back to catch the next citation in this distinguished list, Jack retired for a moment into his own thoughts. He wished he could see her to match up the two parts. That would be neat. Cute kid, for sure. He wondered if he could get to see her the coming winter.

His thoughts wandered back to a recent episode, one of just a few days ago, in which he was the prime mover, but scarcely a heroic figure. If those crazy girls hadn't lugged into the boys' dining room sometime during the night two very small pigs in a crate, everything would have been all right. The girls, or whoever it was—Jack was sure Sally Franz was the instigator—had set the crate on the table belonging to Jack's cabin. On the side of the crate scrawled in big letters was the name of the cabin and, "Us boys want more to eat."

With a skill and caution worthy of better causes, Jack and a crony of his had managed to sneak a sack of chickens into the kitchen of the girls' camp. They had tried to calm these startled fowl and left them roosting doubtfully in the darkness along the edge of the central table. The hens had made a shambles of the kitchen. Also, Jack and his buddy had failed to pick birds that were housebroken.

The cook at the girls' camp, coming in early to start breakfast, had almost quit his job. Nothing but a chance to punish the culprits would satisfy him. When the pair showed up shamefaced after Meeting, the cook had calmed down.

"Listen, boys, you made a mistake. I made mistakes too, when I was a kid. I still do. One of mine is in the cellar right now, a consignment of overripe melons I took not realizing that most everybody would be out on hikes this last week. I had to clean up your mistake. Now you clean up mine. We'll be even. See?"

It was a nasty job, for the cartons into which the boys had to shovel the gooey mess sometimes broke. Jack's only pair of long pants were beyond cleaning. Perhaps sometime he would learn to stop and figure the angles on something before he did it. That's what had got him into trouble at home. Guess he'd had his lessons now, several of them, all unpleasant, during the summer.

Those blasted melons, or rather, those blasted hens, got Jack into trouble all over again the next morning, when his folks showed up to take him home. His mother let out a little squeal of delight, and almost gathered her son into her arms. She stopped in time, noting the distressed look on the boy's face. His father shook his son's hand gravely, surveying him carefully from top to toe.

"You've sure got muscle," he observed. "And what a tan. This pair of shorts your traveling costume?"

"Well," Jack answered lamely, "my shirts are down in the bottom of my trunk. I didn't need them. And my khaki pants got rotten melon on them so I had to throw them away."

"Got what?" his father asked.

"Rotten melon. 'Nother guy and I—we moved a whole load of melons out of the food room for the cook at the girls' camp. They sure were ripe."

"Well," his mother remarked. "It seems to me the camp might hire somebody to do dirty jobs like that."

She opened Jack's trunk to hunt for some shirts, and perhaps a pair of moccasins, since Jack didn't seem to know where his shoes were, either.

Mr. Fox took the opportunity to quiz Jack's counselor, who had just come up to shake hands.

"Jack, will you see if you can help your mother find some proper gear for you? I want to talk with your counselor a moment."

"I can't understand it," the man began, when they were out of ear-shot. "This place has transformed the boy. Good muscle, proud bearing, chin up and all that. But there's something happened inside that kid, something more than just the good tan on the outside. Whatever it is, if it will keep him steady this winter, we'll never be able to thank you enough. Do you think it will last?"

The counselor reflected. "Well, you can't ever be sure with a boy. Boys are complicated. Jack operates on impulse pretty much. He's had some hard knocks this summer, and he's taken them in stride. I think he's learned something from them. I think too, you won't find him quite so taken with the rock-and-roll crowd when he gets home."

"How did you manage that?"

"Perhaps I'm forecasting too much. But the camp, you know, stands for something quite different from rock-and-roll. I think the boy has absorbed the camp ideals. It may kind of put him out of step with the crowd at home. I wouldn't dare predict whether he will stay out of step or not, or whether he'll figure he better get back into step with the school crowd. But still, he's got a mind of his own. He won't be led around by the nose. In fact, he won't be led at all till he decides it's something he wants."

"And you think he's found something he wants?"

"I'd say so. He's got a different slant on things, new values, I guess it is. Anyway, let me know if I'm right, or if I can be of any help."

Mr. Fox took the proffered hand. "I sure will. Three months from now I'll write you how it stuck, all you've done for him. I hope it will be as penetrating a letter as yours to us at midseason."

As to the promised letter, Mr. Fox didn't get around to it, but gratitude finally pushed Mrs. Fox into writing. The letter came in at a low moment for Jack's counselor. It made his day.

"My first reaction when I saw Jack," the letter read, "was one of dismay. The boy looked so uncouth. Uncivilized, I guess is the word. But after all, that was what we wanted, I see, as I think back to those grim days of Jack's trouble at school. We felt that Suburbia had really got him. Now, we're happy to say, the camp has broken its hold. Mr. Fox was afraid Jack would go back to the same crowd he had been with and fall into the same patterns. But Jack stated on the way home that he couldn't see anything in 'that bunch of morons.' Now he's finding new friends of a different type.

"That morning that we picked him up at camp, when he seemed so uncivilized, it wasn't that he was heedless of the feelings of others, as I had assumed, but just that he was so caught up in the ideals of the camp, its ruggedness, its simplicity, its honesty, that while he was under the spell he couldn't understand any other attitude. He still has nothing but scorn for the general softness of the family. The first couple of nights he slept on the floor of the back porch. He was furious when I woke him up one night to tell him it was raining, and the storm might blow in on him. A week later he moved into his room, but still slept on the floor.

"At any rate, if a camp can do this for a youngster, and there are enough such camps, it speaks well for the hardiness of the next generation, despite city living.

"One curious type of sensitivity is Jack's new feeling toward his younger siblings. He has twice now offered ideas for their activities which he thought would build on some talent one of them has and thus 'make the kid feel good inside.' This must come from camp or, more specifically, from you, since the relation between the boys in a cabin and their leader seems to be a very close one.

"I don't want to give the impression that Jack is sprouting wings. Sometimes he can be infuriating. But the difference is now that when we point out something like this to him, instead of putting up the usual kind of unpleasant defense, he comes around and admits he was wrong. My sister who is a psychologist says that only a secure person can admit he's in the wrong.

"I'm sending a copy of this letter to Mr. .... As director, some of the credit must be his, of course, for setting up such an effective atmosphere for young people."

In all honesty, we must admit that the results of a summer at camp, though good, are not always quite that good. Jack is a composite of a number of careless, even callous youngsters. The letter just quoted is also a composite of various items in any camp's postseason fan mail. If a camp can contrive to do even half as much for a given youngster, it stands justified. It has a reason for being.

A camp with a philosophy, with a clear vision of what it wants to achieve and how it proposes to reach these goals can match the changes mentioned in the letter; oftentimes, with a particular boy or girl, can cite transformations even more spectacular.

To the deep-seated insecurities that afflict many urban children, the camp will have offered the healing balm of effort and success in mastering the skills of wilderness living, the self-assurance of new competence in the water, the warm, satisfied sense of having helped with some difficult construction project. The camper will have extended a helping hand to some other youngster. He has been useful. He senses new courage, new self-reliance, and the spirit of adventure, perhaps dormant before.

The sophisticate will have been humbled by the realities of having to wrest shelter and safety from stubborn elements which yield only to skill and perseverance. His gadget-ridden affluence will have shown itself irrelevant in time of need. His softness and consequent timidity will have been replaced by a new strength both physical and spiritual. His uncertain moral standards will have been transformed by the acceptance, perhaps unconsciously, of a whole new set of values, unselfcentered, far reaching, durable. Coming from the superficial relationships of a city, he will have experienced what close living with a small number of individuals can do to reveal the deep interrelatedness of all life. He may even have caught just a glimpse, but an eventually transforming glimpse, of unsuspected foundations, of the primacy of things of the spirit.

His personality will have been made whole, his spirit enriched, his mind integrated. Paradoxically, while he will have been made more sensitive to others, his own individuality will have been assured. Never will he become the conventional, conforming, timid, uncreative stereotype known as the "fractional man" of city crowds. With secure foundations for his own philosophy, he will know what he thinks and why. He will stand on his own two feet and speak out with the courage of honest conviction.

By no means transformed suddenly into a paragon of virtues, as the above recital might seem to imply, a boy or a girl after a season at a good camp may appear at first to have gained in some areas so much as to justify the term "enchantment" as applied to the effect of the camp season on him. But after a while the spell wears off. What seemed at first to be completely changed attitudes toward parents and teachers, toward authority in general, slips back into some of the former hostility. Yet only at times. Down below the returning pettiness of the day, there is a change that endures. The communications gap isn't quite so wide, and there are bridges. Rapport with fine staff at camp has built them. And some of the impatience to satisfy a whim instantly has disappeared. The child has been in contact with the slow, steady processes of nature. He has found what it is to work away at a skill day after day because he wants some coveted goal more than anything else in life. He will also have come to realize that to gain something you must work for it. Life is not a one way street. One must give as well as receive. It involves a reciprocal relation.

Above all, a boy or girl after a season's exposure to the influence of a good camp will show a surer motivation. He may even attack less congenial studies with new purpose. In the deeper application he gives them now, he discovers satisfactions he had missed before. This feeling for new values, even a sense of mission now and then, extends beyond school studies. It infuses all of life. It even seems to establish a dialogue with the future until plans and determination start to emerge.

As with any normal youngster, there will be times of relapse, even long periods when he may seem to drift, and is caught up again in the ebb and flow of the blind but powerful currents surging around him. But something is different. The child does have resources of hidden strength, attitudes built into his very being which protest these currents and resist them.

20

A.D. 2,000, or conversations with the future

If we try to project the surging currents of the present into the decades ahead, we are sure not to like what we see: a warring world, overpopulated, with the violence of decaying cities and the psychoses of urban life spreading and becoming more intense. Will the whole complex structure finally end in the fiery holocaust so often predicted?

Or, let's take another view. Suppose we achieve peace short of the holocaust, or that some part of the globe manages to impose an arbitrary peace on the rest. We've seen this before, the Pax Romana, which established a warless society in the Mediterranean world. For five hundred years this society endured, but the age was sterile, soulless, dead.

"In wildness is the preservation of the world," Thoreau wrote. "We need the tonic of wildness, to wade sometimes in marshes where the bittern and the meadow hen lurk, and hear the booming of the snipe. To smell the whispering sedge where only some wilder and more solitary fowl builds her nest, and the mink crawls with its belly close to the ground."

Will summer camps be able to restore this tonic of wildness to the human race? Will they ever become conscious of the precious gift they can offer, not only the gift of close communion with nature whence we sprang, but the priceless boon of the strengths and qualities of spirit and the attitudes essential to the health of the individual and in a larger sense to the preservation of society?

The slogan of one of the biennial conventions of the American Camping Association was "Better Camping for All." At present, camping of any sort touches a pitifully small proportion of the children of the country.

If camping is good for the children who experience it, then it should be even better for all the children and thus for the nation and the world. As much as we dislike government interference, the indications are that there will be more of it. Legislation for minimal safety standards is probably just a beginning, a beginning caused by the deficiencies of the camps themselves. Every substandard camp poses a threat not only of disaster, of a damaged public image, but of further governmental regulation. We are powerless to do anything about this except as an individual who may have a chance to help some new director set up a safer, more effective organization. In regard to government regulation, we can no doubt, if the American Camping Association continues strong, have a salutary influence on the way new laws are written. At least two types of government or publicly sponsored camping are worth watching.

One is the school camps with which some city education systems are experimenting. This is just a touch of camping, to be sure, but even that much can instill a greater respect for the out of doors, adding to the growing body of conservation-minded electorate. Inasmuch as that period, usually just five days, is augmented by discussion and study before and after the actual experience, it is more effective than just the length of time itself would suggest.

Another type of government-sponsored camping is that partly supported by the various kinds of federal funds available for extending the experience of camping to disadvantaged groups. This is full of promise if it can be guided into patterns of real camping, serving as an antidote to the worst aspects of urban living. Much more in the way of financial support may flow from government sources in the future. It is up to those presently part of the camping movement to guide this effort by making articulate in various ways the best ideals of camping.

It is difficult, of course, to win any far-reaching agreement as to what are the best ideals of camping. The movement means different things to different people. It would seem to the writer, however, that an analysis of the social scene today should lead to the conviction that many of the ills besetting us are the result of urban living. That, therefore, a type of camping which offsets these influences, restoring some of the more austere, primitive living of our ancestors, would be in order. In this time of rising costs, the emphasis in expenditures should be on mature and competent staff, not on buildings and equipment. If we can get this ideal across to government planners and agency directors, we shall have cleared the first hurdle on the way to more effective camping.

The whole implication in the view of camping set forth in this book is the need above all for our nation's children to have more contact with the wilderness. The picture of camping sketched above is also that found in a relatively small institution, where personal relations of a deep and lasting sort may be established.

If camping bears any relation to agriculture, and it does in some ways, it would seem that camps are fated to get bigger, less personal, more efficient in handling larger masses of children. One shudders at the thought. One way out, in which camps can still effect the economies possible with larger organizations, lies in the small unit camp, such as some of the agencies are experimenting with now, groups of forty to sixty children, semiautonomous, quite separate in most ways, yet under the same general direction, the same basic deals and values, with a central office, one coordinated buying plan, and a single promotional budget.

Many people may ask where the wilderness is to be found for all these camps of the future. The prospect will be discouraging unless all who are interested in conservation and in childhood can unite their efforts and their voices to guard what wild lands we still have, preserving them both from the encroachments of selfish commercial interests and from unwise, shortsighted "development" for public use. The "multiple-use" ideal of the federal park system, on first view, seems sensible. But when it is scrutinized more closely it turns out to be a snare and a delusion. Multiple use of wilderness areas means that certain uses hostile to the needs of true conservationists and nature lovers crowd out all else. Trail bikes and snowmobiles are an increasing menace. Ski tows and motorboats are two of the most sickening examples of the rape of the wilderness. Nearly all mountains in some areas are already scarred, their trails cut across by endless tows and lifts. Most waterways are being rendered unsafe for canoes and sailboats by high-speed motorboats. The illusion of wilderness is shattered for all by the noise and the stench of these modern monsters. Both the skiing and the motorboats are fine in their place. We must define their place quickly, before it is too late. The principle must be established of setting aside wider areas for real conservation. This can be done by public action, and also by private combines of conservationists. There are good examples of both today. Such areas will prove to be not only a conservation, a saving of wilderness, but a preservation also of the finest qualities of the nation's youth.

If then, we can become conscious of sociological trends, if we can understand what is happening to our society, and if we can set up patterns in organized camping which are soundly educational, not just adopted because of misguided parental pressure, camping can truly exemplify the description of it given by Charles Eliot of Harvard when he called it America's greatest contribution to education. If camping is truly educational, as it should be, then its importance in guiding our nation's future can hardly be overestimated. Then shall we with good reason rejoice to see the realization of the old slogan, "Camping for All."

Another blessing should emerge from the hoped-for universality of camping. If, as it would appear, religion no longer plays any vital role in our culture, it is still possible for camp directors to foster the basic attitudes of religion, the ethic of the Golden Rule, the sense of wonder which undergirds the vision of the mystics. Much of the present generation rejects religion as being irrelevant. Camping permits returning to the sources whence religious feeling sprang—the sense of awe in the presence of the imponderables, the contemplation of dedication in individuals, the mystery of the spirit as it manifests itself in nature and in people.

Without taking ourselves so seriously as to imply that camping can save the world, let us also acknowledge soberly that we do have a tool of tremendous significance as one of the possible determinants of the course of our culture. If we rise to the challenge as educators in a particularly effective environment, we can have some influence on whether the average citizen of the future is weak, self-indulgent, violent, and purposeless, or strong, outgoing, gentle, the revelation of man's potential in an ideal society.